The Covenant of Marriage

Study Guide

A Guidebook for Couples and Singles

*How to Build the Best Marriage,
the Best Life, and the Best You!*

Mark Johnson, MD and Holley Johnson, MS, RDH

Carpenter's Son Publishing

The Covenant of Marriage Study Guide

©2020 by Mark Johnson

Published by Carpenter's Son Publishing, Franklin, Tennessee

Published in association with Larry Carpenter of Christian Book Services, LLC
www.christianbookservices.com

Scripture taken from THE HOLY BIBLE, NEW INTERNATIONAL VERSION®, NIV® Copyright © 1973, 1978, 1984, 2011 by Biblica, Inc.™ Used by permission. All rights reserved worldwide.

Scripture taken from the NEW AMERICAN STANDARD BIBLE®, Copyright © 1960,1962,1963,1968,1971,1972,1973,1975,1977,1995 by The Lockman Foundation. Used by permission.

Interior and Cover Design by Suzanne Lawing

Edited by Robert Irvin

Printed in the United States of America

978-1-94952025-34-1

Contents

PLEASE READ THIS FIRST

Dear Reader,

If you are reading this, you want a better Marriage. There are likely many things about your husband or wife and your Marriage you are delighted with—which is why you are married. You see wonderful things in another person and you want to build a wonderful life together. In many ways you are doing just that.

So, how can we make it better? The thoughts that guide this study need to be clear up front so you understand what we are trying to accomplish, and why. One approach is to try to make good things better—working on better listening, more consideration, deeper understanding, or more sensitivity. Many resources take this approach. Instead, we want to do something very different.

For decades Mark has been a surgeon. This trained him to approach problems in a particular way. The best surgeons *properly diagnose* and *successfully treat* significant problems. People who sought his care did so because they knew something was wrong. Some knew exactly what—a kidney stone, a prostate infection—and the answer was obvious. But others came with just a symptom. Something did not look right—a little blood-tinge in the urine, or did not feel right—a little pain they never felt before. His job was first to figure out what was wrong. Then to tell the person. Then to do something that hopefully would resolve the issue. Often none of these were straightforward. Some problems are difficult to sort out. Some people did not deal well with the truth, even when stated as tactfully as possible. At times the cure involved something more extensive, challenging and threatening than anticipated.

Over many years working through such issues he gained a deep appreciation for a precise and comprehensive understanding of physical problems, for communicating clearly—if gently—the truth about the problem, and most of all a profound gratitude for the ability to remedy issues that were at times much more serious than anticipated. That tinge of blood in the urine could be a small asymptomatic kidney stone or a cancer that led to removal of a kidney—from which the person fully recovered with no ongoing issues; or a bladder cancer treated by removing this organ and building a replacement out of intestine—which involves a lifetime of maintenance and tinkering. He also noticed that patients, and even physicians, often stop short of exploring a problem to its root cause. Patients want, and physicians may offer, a band-aid for what proves to be a life-threatening, perhaps life ending cancer. The key to the *best outcomes* is to *ask the right questions*. Make sure you find the most important answers, then do the right thing to fix the problem—even if it hurts, or the cure initially seems as unwelcome as the disease. This is the path to the best physical life. Another reality also became clear. In the end it is the person's body and their life. One can offer truth and the path to a better life, but people are free to choose this path or any other.

How does this relate to Marriage if we are trying to build the best one? Holley and Mark's other passion has been building a deep, rich and powerful Covenant relationship with God, and building the deepest and best Marriage possible. We found this surgical mindset to be really helpful to build these relationships. How, and why?

We all have a lot that is good about our Marriage, but there are those other things… Something does not look quite right. Something does not feel quite right. Sometimes these are simple to understand and correct.

We see an answer in Scripture and make a different choice—issue resolved. But there are those patterns, those recurring conflicts, those growing feeling about our spouse we do not want, or maybe that crisis of moral compromise. We can focus on the positive and keep trying to grow that part of our relationship. We may believe we are being loving, gracious, and Godly by ignoring or compartmentalizing whatever does not look right or feel right. And sometimes this works. The problem is not really that serious. We overlook, move on, and continue building. But as we look around and see a 25%+ divorce rate among Christians, we also realize that just putting a bandaid over it and hoping it heals on its own does not always work. What can we impart that would improve every Marriage, and get ones on shaky footing onto solid ground—if, of course, people actually followed the plan?

We discovered something over the decades so important that we want to help everyone understand it. God's plan for our lives and our Marriages is far better than we can imagine. Let's repeat that—in each of our minds, when we think about the best-case scenario for our Marriage, God has a working plan to create something beyond our dreams. We can rock along, row hard, enjoy the good times, bail water out of the boat that comes from all the leaks, and hope the thing doesn't sink beneath us; or we can let God do something He deeply desires to do. We can let Him build, or rebuild, our Marriage His way. Actually, we do the building, but according to His plan instead of ours. If we do this, we will find our Marriage takes us places we never dreamed it would, and builds things within us that allow us to live our best lives. So…how do the nautical theme and the operating room picture come together?

We do not need to fix what works well. We do need to look more carefully at what is not working well. Issues, conflicts, problems, and our unpleasant inner experiences—disappointments, unmet expectations, and many other things—all of these are the doorway to *a problem-solving journey God intends us to take.* We may find what is needed in our Marriage is different from what we thought. God wants to show us the true nature of Marriage and how it is built into the best possible relationship. He wants us to understand our new identity and nature, and how to build the relationship so *both people grow to their God-given potential.* He wants us to learn how to transform those things about ourselves that hold us back from building the life and relationship He intends for us. As you might imagine, this conversation is deeper and more involved than one about how to be nicer to each other. But this conversation and the powerful changes it is intended to produce may be the best things that ever happened to your Marriage. If you agree to open this door and take this journey. These are not our ideas and our plan. These are God's ideas and His plan. We have just proven their amazing benefit.

Happy Reading!

PLEASE READ THIS NEXT

Two people are madly in love, feeling things they have never felt, doing loving things for one another they have never done, convinced they have found "the one" and true love. They want to spend their lives together. So they marry. In their Marriage they want this blissful state to continue till death do us part. And great Marriages do happen.

ALL ARE EQUALLY MARRIED, BUT ALL MARRIAGES ARE NOT EQUAL

But non-great Marriages also happen. Everyone begins in love, determined to make the relationship work, with deepest feelings and highest hopes. Why do some find enduring love, while others find something very different? How does a great Marriage happen? In this study we are going to explore vital lessons from a source you may have never considered—from *the nature of the marriage relationship itself.*

Our culture has lost the historic understanding of Covenant relationships; instead we try to transform marriage into whatever the latest cultural viewpoint says it should be. However, the Covenant of Marriage was the second gift of God to humanity, after life itself. Marriage is found throughout history in every culture, and is largely unchanged through history—until lately. What about Marriage has changed? Marriage is being entered far less often and is failing in unprecedented numbers. Why? Because current approaches are not in synch with the actual nature, structure, and function of this relationship. These innovative and progressive approaches fail to build this relationship to its potential. On the other hand, if we do understand...

...the **underlying reality** that makes the Covenant of Marriage a covenant;

...the **practices and principles** that flow from this underlying reality;

...that marriage is **not just a tie that binds**—instead,

it is **a plan designed by God** to build the **strongest love relationship** and the **best working relationship**, and to **grow and transform** the participants into people capable of building not only good marriages, but good families and good societies...

If we understand these things we are now poised to embark on one of the greatest adventures in life: building a great marriage, and **building the best version of ourselves in the process.** Welcome to the journey, and bon voyage!

My wife Holley and I have a decades-long love-for-a-lifetime Marriage, a relationship built firmly on the underlying reality of marriage, then on everything that flows from this reality. This understanding is the key that unlocks every good thing Marriage has to offer. It also explains much of what goes wrong in Marriages. A Marriage built in accord with these realities turns out one way. If, instead, we try to make marriage *what we want it to be,* that is *out of accord with what it is,* the relationship *will not* be...*cannot* be...built to its potential. We want to share with you what we have learned—how to understand and build the best marriage by following God's plan. In order to fully grasp God's plan, though, we must learn something else first. We must learn *what a Covenant is...and why it is the heart of God's plan for our Marriage and our life.*

WHO DO YOU SEE WHEN YOU LOOK ACROSS THE BREAKFAST TABLE?

The answer to this question may be the most important of all in determining
the ultimate quality of your marriage, and the answer may not be what you think.

LOVE VS. SELF-INTEREST

We are going to examine two things that often compete in a marriage,
but should not—for a reason that may surprise you.

TRUE LOVE...

Is it *found*, or *built*?
Is love-for-a-lifetime something we just fall into?
Or, do we simply find the right person?
True or false: Our heart toward someone over time is most
powerfully determined by how he or she treats us.

ACTIONS...

DIRECTED BY *THE GUIDANCE SYSTEM ACQUIRED FROM OUR CULTURE*
MOTIVATED BY *LOVING FEELINGS*
DIRECTED BY *OUR COMMITMENTS*
Which is the path to building love-for-a-lifetime?

GOD'S GOAL FOR OUR MARRIAGE:

To consistently build, vs. building with one hand while we are neglecting or tearing down with the other.

THE SCRIPTURES ON MARRIAGE AND LOVE:

An impossible to-do list, or God's plan to build the best marriage and life?

COVENANT...

...takes these Scriptures and organizes them into a plan that makes sense—not only what we are to do, but
why, and even *how* we can do all these things. In fact, Covenant—this relationship designed by God—is
the very heart of God's plan for each of us, for our Marriage, and for all of humanity.

THE COVENANT OF MARRIAGE

WHY DOES THE NATURE OF A RELATIONSHIP MATTER?

INTRODUCTION

To truly understand God's Word we must understand the words that are used. But the meaning of some words has changed over time. It is important to understand a word in the way it would be understood by the one who wrote or spoke it. When God uses the terms *Covenant* of Marriage, or *New Covenant,* what do we understand a covenant relationship to be? When asked about Marriage, Jesus looked back to the *original understanding.* Should we not do the same? Christian teaching about the nature of covenants in our day is different from the way this relationship was understood in first-century Israel. And even then, Jesus had to refer back to the understanding originally conveyed by God because His first-century audience also had misconceptions about Marriage. If we want to understand *our* Marriage would it help to do what Jesus said? Should we also consider the original nature, structure and function of this relationship?

The Covenant Series and Study Guides are based on a definition of Covenant which comes from a book referenced by Kay Arthur in her *Covenant* study[1]—*The Blood Covenant*[2], written by H. Clay Trumbull in 1885. Trumbull was a prominent Christian leader, teacher, author, and editor in the last half of the 1800s. He is termed the "Father of the American Sunday School movement" and was a good friend of D.L. Moody. Trumbull examined covenant relationships in many cultures in his day and throughout history, for this relationship is found in many ancient cultures. He identified the common element in three covenants—a blood covenant, the New Covenant, and Marriage. Each is entered by an exchange of identity between the parties. The parties are joined thereafter by a bond of shared identity and nature. Also, the identity—the fundamental nature of each participant—changes when the identity of the other enters them.

God gave us two of these relationships, and likely the third. If these are the same *type of relationship,* anything we learn about one sheds light on the others. God often uses the imagery of Marriage in the Old and New Testaments to describe His relationship with His people. Thus, we can reasonably pool our understanding of all three relationships to better understand all three. We must emphasize that in doing this we are in no way trying to understand Scripture in a new or different way. Instead, we are trying to find the *original understanding* of this form of covenant relationship. If you have read the Covenant Series, you know the New Covenant is a form of Blood Covenant, and you understand that those in Covenant with Christ—the Body of Christ, or the Church—are also in a Covenant relationship with each other. Thus, lessons about Marriage offer insight about our relationship with other Believers, and vice versa. The ultimate goal of these three relationships is the same—love-in-action toward our Covenant partner, Partner, or partners. God created this *form of relationship* with a specific purpose: to develop our capacity to love. If, that is, we properly understand this relationship and follow God's plan to develop it.

IS A COVENANT A FORM OF CONTRACT?

Today many people view Marriage as a type of contract. Current Christian teaching echoes this view, often describing Covenant as a *contract written by God*. Trumbull's examination of these identity-changing Covenants showed that these are *definitely not* contracts. Instead, these are an entirely different form of relationship. Why does this matter? A contract is entered between two separate individuals, only determines *what we are to do and not do*, and is held together only by the continuing agreement of the individuals. No contract can change *who we are at the deepest level*, or *join two together in a bond of shared identity*, as these Covenants do. This may seem an odd thing to discuss, but misunderstanding the nature of this relationship leads to many problems as we try to build our own Marriage, as we will see.

God's intends that two joined in the Covenant of Marriage build many important things in heart and life *through the relationship*. He knows how our hearts and minds are wired, how relationships grow, how personal growth and transformation occur, and what needs to be built within us so we can meet the challenges of Marriage and life. Again, there is no contract which could accomplish any of these things. God designed Covenant to do all of these things and more. But how? What is His plan?

Scripture has many things to say about Marriage, and regarding love in general. How do we view these Scriptural injunctions? Many see these only as a list of things we are to do to the best of our ability. They believe this list represents the entirety of God's plan—here is the contract, these are the terms, do these things. But some items on this list appear to run cross-grain to our best interests and perhaps to our very nature. Thus, people often reduce the list to "just be as nice as possible." Even if we take God's plan seriously, but still see these things only as a to-do list "because God says so," we are poised for frustration. Some items are things we cannot simply decide to do—like love consistently. If this relationship is a contract, it is one we are unable to fulfill. This *mis-reading of God's plan* does not make sense to us, which leads many to look to other sources for guidance to build their most important human relationship.

In sharp contrast, if we understand the Covenant of Marriage everything falls neatly into place. Marriage is not just a tie that binds. It is also a remarkably detailed, powerful, and multifaceted plan, one that is perfectly designed to accomplish all of God's goals for us—if we understand and implement the plan. Instead of a to-do list, what if we realize that God's injunctions are a blueprint for growth and transformation? If we see this, we will also see the genius of God on full display. The very *transformation* and *joining* that occurs as we enter this relationship is *how we become able* to do these things. If I become a new and different person, what about the way I live? Will a new and different being live the same old life, or a new and different life?

Our new self, now joined to another, is the beginning point for every other thing we are called on to do, to be, and to build. Our newly conjoined life is the beginning point for the deepest and most intimate love.

Based on the results of this plan in our own Marriage, Mark and Holley want to convey an urgent message to everyone: God has a plan—and the plan works. We want to share this plan with you!

FOUR ELEMENTS CHARACTERIZE THIS FORM OF COVENANT

*That is why a man leaves his father and mother and is united with his wife, and they become **one flesh**.*
GENESIS 2:24

1.) EXCHANGE OF IDENTITY = NEW BEINGS WHO SHARE AN IDENTITY

In Scripture a Marriage relationship is termed "one flesh." The word translated "one" in Hebrew or Greek does not refer to a singular item, but to two or more things which share a nature or identity. We find this same word in the phrase "God is One" (Galatians 3:20), referring to the Trinity—three distinct beings who are joined by a bond of nature and identity. Each is fully God, all together are God. Each has a distinct personality and role; all share a common identity.

...so that they may be one as We are one.
JOHN 17:11

How does this relate to Marriage? Marriage is characterized by an exchange and merger of identities. It is intended to mirror the Trinity. Marriage also mirrors the relationship between God and the church, which mirrors the Trinity (John 17). Entry into the Covenant of Marriage occurs as the identity of each literally enters the other and remains. Since "my identity" describes the very core of my being, if a new element of identity is added, what happens to *who I am*?

This picture is graphically presented in Scriptures describing the New Covenant, using terms such as "born again" (John 3:3), "new creature" (2 Corinthians 5:17), "new creation" (Galatians 6:15), "our old self was crucified with Him" (Romans 6:6), "buried with Him through baptism into death" (Romans 6:4), and many others. Since the Covenant of Marriage and the New Covenant are the same form of relationship, we can look to New Covenant imagery to better understand *the process involved* in becoming "one flesh," and *the result*—the joining and transformation of natures. The "old" person ceases to exist. A person with a new, altered identity and nature comes into being. In Marriage, the "single me" is replaced by the "married me," but now we understand the true nature of this replacement. Why does this matter?

If we do not understand Covenant, how can we understand the reality described by "one flesh"? The transformation and joining of Covenant are *the foundation for everything* God intends to happen in

Marriage. These realities are *the reason* for everything God tells us to do and be in Marriage; and *how we become able to do and be* these things.

Contemplate this reality for a moment. What does this mean for you?

_____

_____

_____

Who do you see when you look across the breakfast table? Do you see the other person, or do you see a person who is now an extension of yourself, whose identity you share?

_____

_____

How might this matter?

_____

_____

_____

All I have is yours, and all you have is mine.
JOHN 17:10

All the believers were together and had everything in common.
ACTS 2:44

2.) SHARING OF LIFE IN COVENANT

If two share an identity and are joined at the deepest level of their beings, it makes sense that everything in their outer lives is also shared. The historic practices of Covenant reflect this. Each enters a family relationship with the family of the other. What does it mean to become part of the family of your beloved?

_____

_____

_____

There is sharing of assets and debts, friends and enemies. All obligations become joint obligations. There is no more "mine" and "yours," only "ours." This sharing even includes our bodies: *The wife does not have authority over her own body but yields it to her husband. In the same way, the husband does not have authority over his own body but yields it to his wife.* (I Corinthians 7:4) In sum, external lives are completely joined and shared. Is this reality reflected in our culture's view of Marriage? Why or why not?

_____

_____

_____

This sharing applies to more than material things. God intends there to be **mutual sharing in every aspect of life**—there is to be another who sees, knows, understands, helps, builds, shares, appreciates, and cares. This new, conjoined life is to be shared equally and built by collaboration. **Everything about the two is equally important.** What is built is to reflect the real needs, the inherent potentials, and the life-purpose of each. Covenant is the ultimate all-in relationship—each offering all of their attention and strength to the relationship, their total devotion and complete commitment. All the elements of Covenant work together to teach us how to collaborate, and how to build something that most benefits both. But this pooling of resources and abilities is about more than the couple. It is intended to build a family that enriches lives on all sides.

Is the equality inherent in Covenant a feature in your Marriage? Why or why not?

_____

_____

_____

...each one of you must love his wife as he loves himself...
Ephesians 5:33

In everything, do to others what you would have them do to you...
Matthew 7:12

This is my command: Love each other.
John 15:17

3.) LOVE IN ACTION IN COVENANT

In Covenant, we are called first of all to love our husband or wife **as we love ourselves**. The historic practices of covenant include many specific things we are to do. A very similar list is found scattered through Scripture in verses about either Marriage or love in general. A third, similar list is found by compiling the historic vows from Marriage ceremonies. All three sources paint essentially the same picture of how we are to be toward our spouse. The historic practices of Covenant are a beautiful picture of love in action, as are the Scriptures and these vows. But in *the nature of a Covenant relationship* **we learn something else** that is very important: we find not only **what** we are to do, but **why** we are to do these things, and even **how** we can become able to do these things. We are all familiar with the difference between what we should do, or would ideally do, and what we actually do. God has constructed this relationship to help us actually do and be the things that build the deepest love, the best working relationship, and the most satisfying and gratifying experience of Marriage.

Even if we love another as we love ourselves, might there still be a problem? **How perfectly do we love ourselves?**

_____

_____

If we love imperfectly, why?

_____

_____

In Covenant we are presented with **a definition of love beyond our own—God's definition.** Covenant has many elements that **motivate us** to love-in-action, starting with *the love we feel for each other.* But there is more. We will love imperfectly for many reasons. Covenant *motivates us to choose better things—God's version of love, things that build the relationship*—and to do these with increasing consistency. What is our reward for following this plan? Our Marriage gets better and better.

Historically, the primary responsibility of Covenant is to *faithfully love the other in every way*—in thought, word, and deed. It is our highest honor to do so, (and our deepest dishonor to fall short). This reality is reflected in the Covenant of Marriage in vows spoken in our wedding, but these are an abbreviated version of all the things we are to do and be. We vow the fullness of these when we "take each other in holy matrimony." **We commit ourselves to the entirety of God's plan for marriage.** Throughout history vows have been considered the most binding commitment we can make. In our culture there is a…sometimes loose relationship…between commitments made and things that are done. In Covenant, *the nature of the relationship* and the *vows we make* strongly motivate us to actually follow through, to choose to consistently love our husband or wife in thought, word, and deed to the best of our ability.

What does "love in action" look like?

_____

_____

_____

In brief, we are to honor our spouse above all others, we are to protect, provide for, and defend the other as we would ourselves. We are to cherish, be loyal, be devoted—in every way to love the other as ourselves. There are many more aspects of such love. We will cover these in detail in Lesson Four. **God makes it easier to love another as we love ourselves by making the other literally an extension of ourselves.** God is the One who transforms and joins us in Marriage, reflected by the words of Jesus, "…what God has joined together, let no one separate." (Mark 10:9) It is up to us to recognize these realities, and build our new together-life on these things. These are the foundation upon which **consistent love** is built—the foundation for **love-for-a-lifetime**.

Covenant is more than a to-do list, more than a list of terms in a contract we are supposed to fulfill. There is no list that encompasses **what it means to love,** no list of things to do *that can create love.* The overall sense of Covenant is to care about another in the deepest way possible, to use **any resource we have** and **any potential we can develop** in service of our beloved. Covenant is **the ultimate blank check**—whatever you need, whatever it takes, whatever I have, am, or can become. *Isn't this exactly what our hearts want to do when we are head-over-heels in love?* We will do *anything* for our beloved.

What have you been motivated to do by love?

_____

_____

_____

But how can we do **loving things consistently**? For many of us, behavior is driven by our feelings. Feelings change day to day for many reasons. We have good days and bad days. What about how we treat each other? God wants to shift our *guidance system*, the part of us that determines our behavior, from our feelings to a much more stable and constant foundation. This must happen in order to make consistent love a way of life in a Marriage. We all enter Marriage with a guidance system which produces inconsistent behaviors—building one day, tearing down the next. **God's Covenant plan can re-build and re-direct this system so our behaviors become uniformly constructive.** But we must understand this process, and choose to go through it.

What causes love to **grow deeper over time**? Is it not **how the two treat each other**? Is it not *growing respect* for each other, and *deeper trust* in each other—all of which are **a direct result of our choices and our behaviors?** God's plan produces things which lead to deepening love. Is this how love for a lifetime is actually created?

Have you seen behavior impact hearts, then the course of a relationship?

_____

_____

4.) WHERE DO MY BELOVED AND OUR COVENANT FIT INTO MY LIFE?

If the other person occupies the very core of our being, if we freely inhabit each other's lives, if our highest honor is to fulfill every role inherent in Covenant, where does our beloved and our Marriage fit in to our life? There is only one thing more important than a relationship between a husband and wife, and that is a Covenant relationship with God. **Everything else is less important.** Is this easy or hard to live out in your life? Why?

_____

_____

We can view Marriage as getting what we want on our terms, or we can understand that we have received a gift from God **that comes with an instruction manual**. The secret to building the best Marriage lies in *the transformation that has already taken place when we enter Covenant*. But we must understand some other things if we are to make the most of this reality. We must understand that God *knows more about building hearts and relationships than we do.* Therefore, we are wise to listen to Him. He loves us more than we love ourselves or our beloved. **We do well to attend His School of Love.** We want to be loved for who we are. We want to be authentic. How do we *authentically live* out the new being we have become?

What do you think an authentic life would be for you?

_____

_____

_____

We have now become a different creature, a new self now joined to another. So…who are we? **Do we rely on our perception** to figure out who we are? We will perceive some changes within ourselves, but only some. Initially, much that God tells us about ourselves and His plan *must simply be accepted as true.* Later these will be proven true to our satisfaction—by our satisfaction, in fact. We face a task made much more difficult by a culture that teaches us to trust our own perceptions above all. Also, our culture has *inserted much into the guidance system* we use to build our lives and relationships. Some of these ideas cause problems. Yet, this is the guidance system we bring into Marriage. **God's plan is to substitute a solid foundation of truth and a working plan for this cultural mis-direction.** Changing our guidance system is one of the keys to building the best Marriage and the best life.

This first lesson presents an overview of **the historic realities of Covenant.** Going forward we will see how the realities of *this God-created relationship* combine with *elements He created within us, and with truth He offers to us.* This plan ultimately relies on one thing: **our choices.** We must choose this plan as a whole, then in every detail day after day. To make the best choices we must first see *all the big pieces of God's plan* (Lessons 1-4). Then see *how these pieces fit together, and build* according to God's plan (Lessons 5-9). Then, we will look at **the relationship produced** by this plan (Lessons 10-12).

So far, what changes would you like to see in your Marriage?

_____

_____

_____

_____

_____

_____

_____

LESSON TWO

NEW IDENTITY, NEW BOND IN COVENANT
and
PERCEPTION = REALITY or
REVELATION = REALITY?

WHY IS MARRIAGE SUCH A BIG DEAL?

People want many things Marriage offers—deep friendship, someone always there for you, someone with whom to play, work, have sex, even have children—yet there is an oddly widespread and powerful reluctance to marry. This reluctance even has a name: "commitment issues." Most people understand Marriage is a very big deal. But why? Have we begun filling in this blank? But why the fear? People perceive Marriage to be an infringement on *their life*. In fact, Marriage does more than infringe on our old life, doesn't it? For the best of reasons—to give us a new, better one.

Let us think for a few moments about the fundamental reality of Marriage. Who is the person who sits across the breakfast table? Who are you? And why does this matter?

HOW WE SEE OURSELVES MATTERS

Early in Marriage I discovered a curious reality. I loved deeply and wanted to show it. But something pulled on the other end of the rope in a kind of tug-of-war. My desire to do loving things had a **stopping-point,** beyond which I found it hard to go. What was this stopping point? If something I felt *called to do for the sake of love compromised what I **viewed** as my self-interest* beyond a certain point, which priority won? Often my view of self-interest won. Then something dawned on me: in Covenant my *self* changed. If so, **what happened to my self-interest**? Did this also change? Of course. My self now includes my wife. Her interests became my interests, and are now equally important with my own. Things that were important in my single life may be completely out of place in my new life. Thus, what I *felt was important* for my life might actually have no place in my new life. So, I decided to opt for love and ignore this old-life-based resistance. What happened next was fascinating. I became a better friend to my wife as I did things I had been reluctant to do. To my surprise, though, I found that these new things felt like what I wanted to do all along. I just hadn't realized it. These loving things *felt like an authentic expression of me—of my new self.* Based on this new understanding and my new choices, my guidance system—that inner voice that tells us something is right for us or wrong for us—**began to shift.**

How does your view of self-interest impact your decisions about your spouse?

_____

_____

Has our discussion raised questions about your own sense of self-interest?

_____

_____

BEING ONE FLESH MATTERS

We **change how we live** if we correctly understand our new identity. We will shift the ways we think, believe, act, and even how we feel. What about the way we are now *joined to another*? What practical changes flow from this understanding? Let us consider one of these: **accepting each other.**

Is accepting each other ever an issue in Marriage? If you are married, do you ever not feel accepted by your spouse; or do you sometimes have trouble accepting him or her? Do you feel you are somehow *never enough*? There is a close connection between **feeling accepted and feeling loved,** and between **accepting and loving**. We cannot have the fullness of one without the other.

Do you ever not feel accepted in Marriage, or have trouble accepting your spouse?

_____

_____

Do you notice the correlation between feeling accepted and feeling *loved*? _____
What makes you feel accepted and loved; and what makes you feel neither?

_____

_____

We live in a world that says, "You will be *accepted if*, or *loved if*…" We often bring this viewpoint into Marriage. Our behavior does matter, and does impact our relationship—obviously. Some behaviors need to change for best results—on both sides. Things that can range from mildly annoying to criminal. Different misguided behaviors require different approaches. To be clear, some behaviors should not be accepted, period. But some people **use lack of acceptance to motivate others** to do better, or to give them more…and more. Others were told they **cannot be loved because**…, and spend a lifetime *trying to prove they deserve to exist*. But the view of themselves they embraced means **they will never feel they are enough**. There are many issues surrounding acceptance in Marriage. Does it matter how we handle these questions?

_____

Which of these patterns do you see in your Marriage?

_____

_____

...the kindness of God leads you to repentance.
ROMANS 2:4

We love because He first loved us.
JOHN 4:19

In Covenant we are to help each other in every way. One important way is to **help each other become the best version of ourselves.** But how can we do this? Do we most powerfully motivate someone to change by withholding love and acceptance? God shows us a paradox—He accepts us and loves us as we are, but does not want us to remain as we are. We learn to live and love best *in the context of a loving relationship— because* we are loved and accepted. A loving relationship offers **the strongest motivation to become one's best.** Many issues surround this statement, which we will discuss in later lessons. But consider the converse: would the best motivation to learn to love be to experience a *lack of love*? **How does Covenant address acceptance?** The other person *literally inhabits the core of our being.* **We accepted** our beloved *within us,* and were *accepted within them*. So, is our acceptance already a settled question? We were accepted permanently, in the deepest possible way as we wed. **The most beneficial approach to our spouse reflects this Covenant reality.** If someone is literally *part of you,* how could you reject them? Like you would amputate your arm? God created a relationship that can form the ground from which our greatest personal growth can occur, if we follow His plan. Isn't this what we all need?

Does the way your spouse *treats you,* or the way you *feel about yourself,* impact whether or not you are *actually accepted* in your Marriage? How does this matter?

_____

_____

_____

How we deal with counter-productive behaviors is another question, as well as how the couple can develop the best approach to dealing with each other's need to grow and transform. The foundation necessary for all of this is full acceptance of each other—reflecting the spiritual reality of the relationship—and a corresponding commitment to love each other fully, completely, and consistently. We first accept each other as we are, then urge each other forward. **If we grow together, we will grow together.**

PERCEPTION = REALITY OR REVELATION = REALITY?

...for we live by faith, not by sight.
2 Corinthians 5:7

A problem we all encounter with the realities of Covenant is our perception—and its limits. **We perceive these changes only partially, if at all.** One of the most significant issues we confront—in this Study, in our Marriages, and in life overall—is our inability to clearly perceive things that are *spiritual in nature.* The joining of Covenant is something *God has joined together*—a reality just as sure as gravity and the chair you are sitting in—but beyond our ability to directly see, measure, or conclusively validate. Our culture aggressively dismisses anything of a spiritual nature. But **it is only by understanding the spiritual realities superimposed on our natural world that we can make any sense of our world,** for these unseen realities deeply affect the realities we can see—like relationships. What does it mean to "walk by faith"?

Then you will know the truth, and the truth will set you free.
John 8:32

Sanctify them by the truth. Your word is truth.
John 17:17

The mismatch between our perceptions and reality is one of the most common sources of problems in every marriage. **Moving our perceptions into line with the truth**—about the Covenant of Marriage and about who we now are—**is one of the most powerful tools we have to improve our marriages.** But this raises another question: "What source of information can offer **correct information about these spiritual realities?**" Hold that thought, for it is a very important one. For the moment, I am simply going to lay out the realities about Marriage drawn from Scripture, read in light of the historic understanding of Covenant. If **God's truth sets us free, from what are we set free?**

SOME REALITIES OF MARRIAGE

As we consider these realities, pause after each and **share your thoughts** with your husband or wife (if possible) **about what these realities mean for your relationship.**

1. The **identities of a man and woman are exchanged** via **the physical exchange that occurs during sexual intercourse.** This act creates a Covenant of Marriage between the two, regardless of the intent or understanding of the participants…*Do you not know that he who unites himself with a prostitute is one with her in body? For it is said, "The two will become one flesh."* (I Corinthians 6:16). Historically, we publicly celebrate this Covenant, then have intercourse for the first time on the wedding night to create it.

_____

_____

_____

2. Once this joining occurs, **the two now become a reflection of the Trinity,** the author of this relationship. The two remain distinct in some senses—with personalities, needs, and capabilities unique to each—but are joined by a bond of shared nature and identity. This may be reflected by changing the wife's last name—a deeply symbolic act, for one's name has always been associated with one's identity—as well as in legal matters, such as joint ownership of property. If the Trinity are all God, what are two united in Marriage? They are a *family*. **How do you see your family? Why did God made you two to reflect Himself?**

_____

_____

_____

3. This exchange of identity creates a **new identity for each.** New identity = new creature, new nature, new life. This language is used explicitly to describe what happens when entering another closely-related covenant, the New Covenant. Much of Scripture is written assuming we understand certain words and concepts. Things widely understood at the time these Scriptures were written did not need exhaustive explanation. But 2,000 years later, some of these do require explanation, like Covenant relationships per se. How does the reality of Covenant impact your view of your Marriage? **What opportunities do you think your new life offers you?**

_____

_____

_____

4. The identity/being/nature/life that defined us prior to Marriage no longer exists once we are married. **The *single* me is replaced by the *married* me.** This change brought about by Marriage is far more than a legal distinction involving a license. It is a spiritual reality which impacts every aspect of our being, every aspect of our life, and every aspect of the relationship we now have with the love of our life. What impact do you think God intends this change of identity to have? We spoke of things

brought forward from the old life that do not fit in our new life. If you noted some of these things, **what should replace these things in your new life?**

_____

_____

_____

5. Think about how you started out in life, when your identity was first present on earth. You were a single cell with a unique combination of nucleotides in your DNA—three billion or so unique pieces of chemical data in an order never before seen. At this point you contained every potential you will ever have. But how much of this potential was expressed as a visible creature, impacting other people and the world? So it is with the new creature we have become. We obviously bear many similarities to the person we have been—athletic potential, brainpower, artistic talent, and other things. But we are new and different in other ways. You started as a cell that grew into a body with unique DNA, but you are also a distinct conscious being who will exist for eternity even when separated from this DNA-directed physical body that has grown around you. It is at this deeper level, **the spiritual level, that our identity is altered and joined by Covenant.** Over time, you will see evidence of things shared with your husband or wife. Some are amusing, others important. And you will see new elements which reflect the "new you." **Which of these new things within you are part of God's plan for your best future?**

_____

_____

_____

6. Another truth I want to begin discussing is **the difference between our true self—our identity— and the optional add-ons** that accumulate within on our journey through life. There is a part of us that needs to be unconditionally accepted—and is to be once we are joined in Covenant. Then, there are parts of us we _also think of as self, as part of our identity,_ that are NOT part of our actual identity—such as habits, preferences, and character qualities—aspects of which can damage relationships. These in turn reflect ideas—that form beliefs, values, goals, and priorities—drawn from our culture or other sources, ideas we embraced. And, as we will see, ideas we can un-embrace. For now, think about **who you are.** Who have you become in the Covenant of Marriage? Also, what might it mean to be confused about who you are? We all spend our lives trying to figure out who we are, and may get only a partial answer over a lifetime. So, **how do we know we have found the right answer?** Our goal is to live an _authentic life._ We want our lives to accurately reflect who we are in the core of our being. All of us want the unique being we are to impact the world, and leave behind something significant. We want our lives to have meaning and purpose. **All of these can only flow from our true identity, and only occur as we express our true nature.** Authentic lives create satisfaction and gratification that occur in no other way. For posers, or those somehow forced to live out of accord

with their nature, such satisfaction is impossible. A deep and intimate relationship requires that we first know the truth of our deepest being, then share this true self with another. But there are voices in our schools, our media, our culture, our families, and even in our churches that misinform us about who we are. This mis-information may or may not be intentional and malicious—as some of our cultural influences certainly are—**but misinformation about our self always robs us of a piece of the abundant life God intends for us. Where are you in your journey of self-discovery?**

_____

_____

_____

7. Our **optional add-ons** are *decisions we have made* about values, priorities, preferences, and goals. These form our view of many things, such as: the best life, the things most desired, the things to be avoided, and the path to our best life. These also **largely form our character**, the overall way we approach life—the things others expect of us and the things we expect of ourselves. These also **form our guidance system**. Can you distinguish between your authentic self—your true identity—and optional add-ons? We ultimately **want to identify all the add-ons that cause problems in our Marriage.** See how many add-ons you can identify and list at this moment.

_____

_____

_____

LESSON THREE

SHARING OUR "TOGETHER LIFE" IN COVENANT
and
THERE IS A LEARNING CURVE...

Now I know in part; then I will know fully, as I am fully known.
I Corinthians 13:12

Mommy, Daddy, WATCH ME!! From the very beginning we want to share our lives with another. We want **to be observed**—for someone to **appreciate what we do** and **care about our lives**. For Holley and me, even the most mundane things we do together have meaning—because we share them. Things we do out of each other's sight have less meaning because these are not shared. As adults, we want to be known and appreciated for *who we are*, then for the life we build from this core. Marriage offers a unique vantage point for us to observe and appreciate each other.

Whoever desires to be great among you shall be your servant.
Matthew 20:26

In Marriage, though, we are **not to be passive observers.** We are to offer any help possible toward the other's efforts. We are to pool resources, freely share talents, gifts, and abilities...and develop our character and capacities so we can be of more help.

List some efforts you have made **to enhance the life of your husband or wife**.

_____

_____

_____

What no eye has seen, what no ear has heard, and what no human mind has conceived—
the things God has prepared for those who love him.
I Corinthians 6:9

Now to Him who is able to do far more abundantly than
all we ask or think, according to the power at work within us.
Ephesians 3:20

This goes beyond advancing the personal agendas of each party. We are now part of something bigger than ourselves, and are to devote ourselves to building our new "together life" by following the plan of God. This life will be more deep, rich, broad, and fruitful than either individual life could be. After decades of following God's plan—never perfectly, but substantially—we bear witness of many wonderful things we never imagined would be part of our lives. Our lives are truly abundant in every sense of the word. What evidence of the power of **God's "one flesh" plan** have you experienced?

_____

_____

_____

God's goal is that **two freely inhabit each other's lives and build something beautiful together.** *This is exactly what falling in love drives us toward*—opening hearts and lives to each other—and what building a relationship that leads to Marriage looks like. But there is a problem we have all seen, even if we are not clear about why this problem exists. When we are falling in love the other person is perfect. We can't wait to tell everyone we know how perfect he or she is. We begin opening up our lives to each other, and things go really well…for the most part. Well enough to keep the love alive. Well enough to give our lives to each other in Marriage. But perhaps not well enough to totally entrust everything in our lives to this person. The over-optimism of the crush fades, replaced by experience that is usually good but sometimes painful.

What happens next? Or, do we make peace with this reality, and share only parts of our lives? Or, do we hold on to our dreams for what the Marriage could be and set out to remake our spouse into the man or woman of our dreams—and settle for nothing less? Or, do we realize **God has a plan for starting where we are, but not leaving us where we are?** Is it just possible that the core of this plan is **not** *changing our spouse* into the Mr./Mrs. Wonderful we desire them to be, **but growing ourselves and transforming ourselves into the Mr./Mrs. Wonderful that we can be for our spouse?** Which is the same thing as *building our way of life* in accord with the new person we became when we wed. Which of these best describes *your* approach?

_____

_____

Though two people start deeply in love, *some do not grow this love for a lifetime.* We want to care and we want to share, but obstacles predictably stand in our way on the path to love-for-a-lifetime. We want to build our Covenant life together into the beautiful picture of collaboration God planned for us. To do this, though, we need to recognize and overcome obstacles we *bring into the relationship* as parts of our personal guidance systems, and even our *beliefs about Marriage*. Is anything in your Marriage **driving you apart?**

_____

_____

_____

Why do you believe these issues exist?

_____

_____

It is **literally impossible** for two people to come together and build a *together life*—sharing *all of life*—without some **deep internal changes**. We cannot engineer this transformation in our spouse—nor are we intended to. If we understand what is needed to build this life we will find we have our hands full with our own building and re-building process. This is a step-by-step, slow and steady path of growth and transformation that God intends to continue for the rest of our lives. Do you believe it is possible that this plan, if embraced by both in a Marriage, can lead to the Marriage of your dreams—and more? Why or why not?

_____

_____

_____

Can you envision this happening in your Marriage? _____

Two hearts in love align with God's plan, *driving more and more loving actions*. At least when we are "feeling the love." But our ***ideas and habits often pull in another direction***. All growing relationships are a dance of pulling together, pulling back, then pulling together. In order for a Marriage to become what it can be we must **build on things that draw us closer,** and we must **put away things that drive us apart.** This "putting away" is one of the key goals of God's plan. We will see how this is done in Lesson Eight. In contrast, we see those who do not follow God's plan often pulling farther apart, ending up in a frustrating stalemate or a cold war, or a hot one that blows their Marriage apart. We have all heard the Scripture: "Love never fails" (I Corinthians 13:8). But can love overcome all the destructive things people do to each other? The outcome of many relationships suggests that it does not. However, **God's plan can remove these destructive things,** if followed.

Do you understand yet how God can do this?_____ If not, stay tuned…

We discussed the historic practices of Covenant: Family relationships now extend to both parties. Every part of life is fully available to both parties and fully owned by both, including assets, debts, obligations, and opportunities. There are no secrets, no hidden places. The conjoined life is to be built by collaboration—about the directions life is to take, what is to be built, and who will be responsible for different parts and pieces.

How does your Marriage **reflect this kind of collaboration?**

_____

_____

In what ways **would you like** your Marriage to reflect this kind of collaboration?

_____

_____

_____

What needs to happen for this to occur?

_____

_____

THERE IS A LEARNING CURVE ON THE WAY TO THE "TOGETHER LIFE"

Clothe yourself with compassion, kindness, humility, gentleness, and patience.
Bear with each other and forgive whatever grievances you have against each other.
Colossians 3:13

There is a learning curve on the way to this together-life. Let's share some predictable struggles we all face along the way, and God's plan to deal with these. Though Covenant suggests that everything is to be fully open to both, that our life together be a communion-fest, what problem might this create? Two people on the way to learning how to love in word, thought and deed **may not be there yet** in key ways. Simply put, **we can be dangerous for each other**. We need to learn how to live this open and communal life. If we turn loose the other person in every part of our lives, he or she may be anything from unsupportive to a wrecking ball. While God's intent is that lives be shared, we must also prove we are worthy of this trust. Our hearts and actions must become truly accepting and supportive. My spouse's problems are also my problems.

Do you feel your spouse would be a **constructive influence** if every aspect of your life were opened to him or her right now? Why or why not? What would need to change for your spouse to be a constructive presence throughout your life? And what would need to change for you to be a constructive influence throughout your spouse's life?

_____

_____

_____

There is a way that appears to be right, but in the end it leads to death.
PROVERBS 14:12

Out of the same mouth come praise and cursing. My brothers, this should not be.
Can both fresh water and salt water flow from the same spring?
JAMES 3:10-11

Let your conversation always be with grace, seasoned with salt, so you may know how to answer...
COLOSSIANS 4:6

Based on prior cultural training we have often **weaponized our expectations, criticisms, and dissatisfaction** as a way of life. We may build with one hand, but neglect or tear down with the other even when dealing with the love of our life. This may be the only *life we have ever known.* The solution in our minds is **finding true love**—which we want to *enjoy* but *may not understand how to build.* We live in a very unloving world. Getting what we want and need, while keeping up a wall of protection (often truly needed), bleeds over into the way we act in Marriage. Though our behavior on the front end of a love relationship is guided by love, **in the end we predictably revert to treating each other as we have always treated other people.** How might this be a problem?

_____

_____

Here is one problem. The way we feel about each other in the long run and the quality of the relationship we build is directly related to how we treat each other. If we act in destructive ways—which we all do—relationship is damaged, often far more than we perceive. A wedding ring does not alter this dynamic. Relationships are resilient, but only to a point. The main point is to build the best Marriage, not to inflict needless damage. God's Covenant plan meets us where we are as we enter Marriage. It is designed to start where we are, then grow us and transform us into people who can freely and constructively inhabit every area of our life together and jointly build this life.

What would need to happen for you to be a more constructive influence in every part of your husband or wife's life?

_____

_____

Do not conform any longer to the pattern of this world, but be transformed by the renewing of your
mind. Then you will be able to test and approve what God's will is—His good, pleasing, and perfect will.
ROMANS 12:2

We come into Marriage already very capable, with a concept of what the end-product is supposed to look like. Consider for a moment *why Jesus spent three years living 24/7 with a group of people.* **What was He doing** all this time? God was **adjusting beliefs, viewpoints and expectations** to equip these people to carry out His plan. God has His own plan for our life together—both challenges and opportunities. To make the most of this life **things must be built**—within each of us and within the partnership—that we may not even be aware we need. His training process is called "doing life together," and it will bring all manner of things our way. Consider for a moment how it changes things for God to make us new creatures and join us at the deepest level as we approach this life. How will this alter the way we deal with the different needs, viewpoints, priorities, expectations, goals, approaches, and strategies we each bring to the table? **Is our "together life" an ongoing competition, or...**

How do you think God intends the realities of Covenant to impact **the way a married couple faces challenges?**

_____

_____

_____

Beyond all these things put on love, which is the perfect bond of unity.
COLOSSIANS 3:14

For Holley and me, our Covenant means we are no longer two people **determined to be right or get our way**—believing that this is the path to glory. The key is **not to be right, but to get it right.** We are no longer adversaries in any sense—instead we are **allies in every sense.** Our differences are not threatening—**these offer strength to the team. Differences are opportunities** for synergy, for us to become greater than the sum of the parts. One must realize that **one's win is not the other's loss**, one's strength **does not** threaten the other's agenda. Instead, a win for one is shared, a benefit to one **benefits both.** The only question is, "What is the path to the greatest joint benefit?" There is no more **"mine" and 'yours,"** only **"ours."** This mindset does more than subtract vast amounts of conflict and discord. The collaboration that replaces competition **builds hearts toward each other.** We are both mindful of what is **truly important to each other, and truly care about the needs of both.** This is the beauty of being *one flesh.*

How do you **deal with conflicting agendas and opinions** in your Marriage? Are you satisfied with your approach? Why, or why not?

_____

_____

_____

What might Jesus need to adjust in us, like the things He needed to adjust in His disciples, for us to succeed in the life and Marriage He plans for us? **First, our view of Marriage really matters.** If we do not enter Marriage with an understanding of Covenant, our goal for Marriage **can only be "value-added to my life."** We want to draw good things from the other person, and offer them some of our own. But we remain—at least in our minds—two separate people joined together only by a bond of agreement—a contract. The point of entering this contract is *my life, made better.* At the same time, in this way of thinking, we share from our life **only what we want to share**. We offer **only what we want to offer.** We only promote the things we want to promote—again, viewed through the lens of a lifetime of carefully-honed beliefs about self interest. *We own our life*, the other merely borrows from it. We bring these ideas for relationship to the table even though we love each other deeply and want to share our lives with each other. We are just very selective about what that looks like.

Whose life is it? *My* life, or our life? What is your view, and how does your view impact your Marriage?

_____

_____

_____

Is God laying any changes on your heart right now?

_____

_____

_____

WHY WE TREAT OUR WIFE OR HUSBAND AS WE DO

Since the ways we treat our wife or husband are so critical, let's take a closer look at why **we treat people as we do**. This equation looks complicated, but it boils down to something very simple: **our choices**. Some behaviors are **in-the-moment choices**. Do we arrive on time, or to keep doing something we enjoy—and be late. Other behaviors do not go through the "conscious choice" circuit. Some are **habits**. Others are **behavior patterns driven by our character**—such as attitudes or feelings. These in turn arise from values, beliefs, priorities, goals, or other **things we have embraced as our personal guidance system.** These things are so deeply ground into the fabric of our being that they feel more like "who we are" than something we have chosen. But in truth each of these elements is a choice we made at some point in our past.

Many elements of our character are **not intrinsic parts of our being**—our identity. Instead, these are **optional add-ons.** If we are to build the best and most loving Marriage we must learn a remarkably important lesson: *some elements of our guidance system and our character* **are the enemy of the best Marriage and our best life**. Yet we resist changing these things because it *feels like* changing them would be like cutting off our arm. **We say, "That's just who I am!"** But in reality these things eat away at relationships, Marriage, and ourselves—even though we were persuaded at some point that *our self-interest is advanced by these things.* However, if these things translate into unloving behaviors that damage our Marriage, that hurt one who is now a part of us, *these things are the enemy of our soul*, and we must deal with them as such.

What optional add-ons within you are the *enemy of your soul?*

_____

_____

Here is **one more evidence for the genius of Covenant.** We resist amputating the optional add-ons we have been discussing because **these feels like genuine expressions of our identity.** But what has Covenant done? It *changed our identity and the way we are connected to another.* Part of God's motivation to get us to shift toward consistently loving behaviors is **realizing that these consistently loving behaviors are now the most authentic expression of who we have become.** If we compare our sense of self-interest (for a being who no longer exists) with God's invitation to authentically express our new being, don't we want authenticity?

We must recognize the vital importance of this process of growth and transformation, and **actively participate in the process God designed to accomplish these things.** God wants us to learn to build with both hands—actually, in a Marriage, with all four hands. In the next section we will begin to examine these processes. For now, just **consider God's goals for your married life.** Realize that God's plan requires adjustment by both people. Realize that His goal, and everything He directs us to do, is designed to **build the most loving relationship and the best life experience.** He wants us to grow—from the love we *know how to display* to loving well and deeply across the spectrum of life. Whatever this requires of us is well worth the cost in light of the outcome.

GOD'S COVENANT PLAN

God's plan is to weld our lives as firmly together as He has *welded our identities.* To do this, He created hearts capable of love—to energize and reward love. He offers us His definition of love to replace our own. Then, He uses the vows of Marriage to shift our guidance system from in-the-moment feelings to our commitment—to love consistently according to His definition.

As we wed, He transforms us into a new creation. He instructs us to grow this new creation to maturity. He instructs us to be transformed by the renewing of our minds—to revise our guidance system for behavior from the counter-productive things learned from our culture to His truth. This guidance now aligns perfectly with our new nature, God's definition of love, our vows, and the Word of God. God's plan merges the deepest longings of our hearts, the way love grows, the way relationships develop, the ways love is shown in action, and the rewards of a loving and authentic life. His plan combines all these together to build a deep and intimate Marriage, and something called the "abundant life." *May you have one of each!*

What life do you believe this plan could build for you?

_____

_____

_____

_____

_____

_____

LESSON FOUR

LOVE IN ACTION IN COVENANT
and
THE VOWS OF MARRIAGE

How many of us like it when we are **supposed to do** something we **do not want to do?** Where's the fun in that? Isn't *having a good time* and *doing what we want to do* pretty much the same thing? In Marriage, don't we want most of all to have a good time? Isn't success in any realm about having things our way, and doing what we want? In everything that really matters, though—in career, sports, music, art, and many other realms—**don't we first need to learn what to do and how to do it?** Talent and creativity, plus understanding, plus discipline lead to success. The phrase, **"do what you *need* to do, so you can do what you *want* to do"** applies to many things in life, including one of the highest-skill, most complex tasks we will ever face—building a good Marriage. Do we choose a heart surgeon who took the Do-What-You-Feel-Like-When-You-Get-In-There training course on-line? He's cheaper, and I'm sure things will all work out just fine… Or, if a person is holding your heart in his or her hand, would you rather have a surgeon who is fully trained to take the best care of your precious organ?

THE ROLE OF THINGS WE SHOULD DO IN A MARRIAGE

If we are married, or thinking about it, we are feeling a lot of love and doing vast numbers of loving things for our beloved. **Isn't this enough? Yes**…if that is all we feel and all we do. But this is never the case, especially over time—over years of Marriage. So… what is it we need to do? To build the best Marriage, on occasion we must *do things we do not feel like doing, and not do things we feel like doing.* Why? Simply put, **to have the relationship we want we cannot always do what we want.** We can have it one way or the other. We can't have it both ways. O.K. So, what are these things we need to do because we *should*? What is God's plan here?

You have stolen my heart…How delightful is your love…Your lips drip sweetness as the honeycomb…
SONG OF SOLOMON 4:9-11

God wants us to feel the love, for these feelings energize us to do loving things. He wants us to luxuriate in loving things done by another. He wants us to experience the joys of giving and receiving. **He also wants to shift our guidance system.** He wants the loving things we do to arise, not just from loving feelings, but *from a plan we are following to build the best Marriage.* Note what this is *not*: a list of things we should do *"because I say so"*…signed, God. Instead, each of us receives an invitation to attend The School of Love, from a Teacher who knows much more than we do about building relationships. Don't we first need to know what to do and how to do it? Can you think of anyone better to learn from?

Have you ever been involved in an intensive training process? Why did you submit to this process?

Love does no harm to a neighbor. Therefore love is the fulfillment of the Law.
ROMANS 13:10

We have spoken several times of *love in action.* What does this mean? To understand loving or unloving things we must first understand **how these are measured**—and it is not *how we feel while doing them.* Things truly loving are *truly beneficial*, not just an expression of good intentions. It is about the effects a given word or deed has on another. Since we cannot see all of the consequences of an action, we need help making these distinctions. **This help is freely available**, though we may need to make some effort to seek out a specific answer. This help comes **from the Scriptures.** In these God assigns many things to moral categories—some things are **right**, others are **wrong.** *We must understand the importance of this designation and the reasoning behind it.* These are not arbitrary designations motivated by a desire to ruin our good times. And these do not depend on the context: adultery is always wrong. God's statements reflect the ultimate impact these things will have on ourselves and others: think, "**nourishing**" versus "**poisonous.**"

We want to be **treated** with perfect love. Yet, we imagine we have **a right to act in unloving ways.** We think *true love* is the other accepting us and everything we do. If both people are doing damage, and expect each other to embrace these damaging behaviors, what happens next?

"My thoughts are not your thoughts, and my ways are not your ways," declares the Lord.
ISAIAH 55:8

As you consider the list of things termed right or wrong in Scripture, carefully note the difference between where God draws this line, and where this line is drawn by our culture or by each of us. Why this difference? Why is God's guidance system different from our culture's, or our own?

Whose guidance system do you believe is best for you—your own, our culture's, or God's?

How can you actually be *consistently guided* by the one you choose?

_____

_____

Don't worry if you cannot answer this now. We will show you this part of God's plan.

> *Do not be deceived. God cannot be mocked. A man reaps what he sows.*
> Galatians 6:7

Throughout our lives we try to figure out what is right or wrong for us. Our whole culture is doing the same thing. **But based on what?** On what we hope is true? Instead, "right" and "wrong" are moral terms which mirror God's moral distinctions in Scripture, which in turn mirror His moral universe. These distinctions are not arbitrary; **they have to do with all the consequences of an action—with long-term outcomes, with overall benefit to others, or ultimate damage done**. From our limited vantage point we cannot see all of these things. All of humanity together cannot see into the future, to understand the long-term effects of our actions. **We need God's** help to see deeper within ourselves, into others, and into the future if we are to make the best choices.

> *But the one who looks intently into the perfect law that gives freedom, and continues to do this, not forgetting what he has heard, but doing it—he will be blessed in what he does.*
> James 1:25

To better understand this distinction **it helps to use other terms for these categories.** We could use practical terms—constructive or destructive, help or hurt, wound or heal. Or, we could use a pair of terms that relate to our discussion about Covenant: loving and unloving. **Loving things are good, right, constructive, helpful, healing, and based on truth. We are to do loving things…consistently.**

> *If anyone, then, knows the good they ought to do and doesn't do it, it is sin for them.*
> James 4:17

> *You will know the truth, and the truth will set you free…everyone who sins is a slave to sin.*
> John 8:32, 34

There is a similar correlation between violations of God's Word, lies, deception, things that do harm in the long run, things that damage relationships, things that violate our Covenant—and unloving things.

We may not always feel like doing loving things toward our spouse, but are there good reasons we should do these things *anyway*, regardless of how we feel?

_____

_____

_____

Compare your thoughts about this with God's plan to motivate us and enable us to love.

COVENANT IS NOT JUST A RELATIONSHIP—IT IS A PLAN

God designed Covenant as more than a relationship. Covenant is also a wonderfully complex and multifaceted plan, designed to teach us, motivate us, and transform us into people who can learn to love, and learn how to build the best Marriage. Overall, this plan has three parts.

...for I gave them the words You gave me, and they accepted them.
JOHN 17:8

INFORM

God makes it easy for us by to love our beloved by setting our hearts on fire for each other. In this state of mind and heart **we love as best we can.** We want to show our love and learn how to show it more. We want to know everything about our beloved, and get to know love itself (for this is often unfamiliar territory). Scripture first tells us to love another as we love ourselves, and Covenant makes the other part of ourselves. **God's next step is to lay out His view of love**—love in action, things with the best outcomes. We see God's view of love in the moral injunctions in Scripture, in the historic practices of Covenant, and in the vows historically made in a wedding. We can best understand *what we are to do*, and *why we are to do* these things by studying all three sources. Is your understanding of love changing? In what way?

_____

_____

...teaching them to obey everything I have commanded you.
MATTHEW 28:20

Why do you call me, "Lord, Lord," and do not do what I say?
LUKE 6:46

CONFORM

As always, **we are presented with a choice.** We can do what we have always done and do what we want to do (much of which is good and constructive, by the way—haven't we just built the most on-fire love affair in human history?). But we want to know more, to love more deeply and more consistently. We also want to join our life and our future to another. In a wedding ceremony **vows are spoken**. These are always an abbreviated selection of items from a much larger list. This list in its entirety mirrors the Scriptural injunctions on love and Marriage very closely. These vows also perfectly reflect the underlying reality of Covenant and the principles of Covenant.

This is our chance. **We have just vowed in our wedding that we will do all of these loving things, and nothing else.** Even this list is not our entire obligation. **Instead of a list, Covenant is the ultimate blank check.** The correct answer is, **"Whatever you need, whatever I have, whatever I am…or can become."** This is the answer love gives, and this is the answer Covenant gives. What answer do we give?

As noted earlier, many behaviors are simple **in-the-moment choices.** We make these choices for **reasons that are sufficient for us in the moment.** If a given choice works from our perspective, we repeat it. These chosen things become our guidance system. These become part of *what we assume to be true* about our self, our life, and how to best live our life. If we pay attention to all that God says about love in Scripture and in our wedding, **we now have a different set of reasons to make many new choices** for our behavior. Our loving heart offers strong motivation to do more and more of the loving things we learn about. We may not feel confident that **God's guidance is the right move in a situation.** But when we love as God directs and see good outcomes, we gain confidence in God's plan. So, our motivations to conform to God's plan include the good outcomes of doing so, the authority of God's Word in our lives, and our own commitment to do all of these things.

WHAT IS A VOW?

Throughout history a vow has been understood as **the most binding obligation one can make.** Our culture maintains a loose connection between words and actions, but through history in most cultures **fulfilling a vow is seen as the highest honor**, and failure to do so as the height of dishonor. In a wedding, abbreviated vows do not limit our responsibilities, for we also vow to "take each other in holy matrimony." **We sign up for God's Covenant plan in its entirety.** Also, if we vow *to do*, we are also vowing not to do the converse. By vowing our honesty we also commit to not lie, for example. The bottom line? We are expected to fulfill the commitment we make as we enter Covenant.

How do you feel about *conforming* to your vows?

_____

_____

Do not conform any longer to the pattern of this world, but be transformed by the renewing of your mind. Then you will be able to test and approve what God's will is—His good, pleasing, and perfect will.
ROMANS 12:2

TRANSFORM

As we noted earlier, *some elements* of our behavior and our overall approach to other people and life are simple choices. Much will be gained in our relationship by making better choices more often. This puts us on the path to building a *much better* Marriage. But what about **the parts of our guidance system that are not conscious choices?** What does Covenant say and what can Covenant do about these things?

First, let us be clear—we are not talking about changing what is working. **We are talking about ongoing points of conflict and dissatisfaction.** There may be recurring negative patterns in our life that we blame on others, that instead are us unconsciously sabotaging our life and Marriage. Issues may arise from our feelings, attitudes, values, priorities, life goals, and character. To resolve these issues and change these patterns we must do more than change an in-the-moment decision. We must change something deeper within ourselves. How do we know when this is needed? God has issued us an instrument with an alarm that goes off when change is needed. The instrument is our beloved. The alarm is conflict over issues in the relationship that are beyond minor annoyances. When both blame the other for a lack of love, each should look to transformation for the solution.

Is there anything about your life or self you would like to have *transformed*?

_____

_____

_____

THE VOWS OF MARRIAGE

Wedding vows through the centuries contain a rich collection of the elements of Covenant love. These vows simply articulate the *logical consequences of the central realities of Covenant*—the new creatures we have become, now in a one-flesh bond. A selection of these vows are listed, then words within the vows are defined. Since we are all in different places in relation to God's view of love, we will not pose specific questions. Instead, **as you read through, underline areas of improvement for yourself, put parentheses around areas of improvement for your spouse, and circle things that each of you do well.** We hope this will continue to be a useful reference as you address issues and build your Marriage.

Select one item per week. Decide how to best live it out, then do so.

Below is a synopsis of "100 Traditional Wedding Vows," posted on the website Wedding Paper Divas (3). How many elements of Covenant you can identify among these vows?

Before God and this congregation I take you to be my husband/wife; leaving everything previous behind, giving every aspect of myself to you; From now we shall be as one until death do us part; no more I, only we; This ring symbolizes our covenant; I am your beloved, you are mine; I am your friend and you are mine; As the Trinity represents three in one, so do we now, united in marriage, represent two joined as one; and as we are in Covenant with each other and with God, thus three are united by Covenant. I therefore vow: to love, honor, and cherish you; unceasing faithfulness, undying devotion; protection, provision, trust and trustworthiness, perseverance, purity, honesty, charity, kindness, patience, gentleness, and self-control. Where my strength fails and growth of character is needed, I vow to seek the Lord for all that I am not, and by His grace and power grow into the (man/woman) He desires me to be, that I may love you more perfectly. I further vow: to prefer you before all others and to forsake all others; to be yours and yours alone; to share all things, bear your burdens and sorrows, rejoice with you, comfort you, in sickness and health, in poverty and wealth, and in all circumstances and situations to be true to my Covenant vows to you before God.

DETAILS AND DEFINITIONS WITHIN THESE VOWS

It may be helpful to look at the full meaning of each vowed item, so we can clearly understand what we are committing to do and be. Only then can we compare ourselves in relation to them. Specific verses for each item are provided, to emphasize that these also represent God's desire for us. Due to the number of these, we will only cite the reference. Please review these Scriptures and their context as you consider each item.

The following definitions were compiled with the aid of the Merriam-Webster online Dictionary (4). Scripture references are drawn from those that pertain specifically to Marriage or to love in a more general sense. Anything said of love toward a brother or sister in Christ or toward humanity in general would be even more important for our husband or wife. In Marriage we owe each other the very highest standard of behavior.

1.) **Leave** family of origin, friends, and all of one's past behind, **to join together** with another person **to become two new creatures in a new entity—a family.**

   Genesis 2:24; Psalm 45:10; Malachi 2:14-15; Ephesians 5:31; John 17.

2.) This joining is a **lifetime commitment**, a permanent joining.

   Mark 10:9; Matthew 19:6; Romans 7:2-3; I Corinthians 7:39; Proverbs 2:17-19; I Corinthians 13:8.

3.) The other party and **you are now "us" with no part of life or self held back.** Every part of life is open to one another; nothing is concealed.

   Genesis 2:22-24; Mark 10:8; I Corinthians 6:19-20, 7:2-5.

4.) **Love and friendship** are pledged in their fullest possible definitions.

   Song of Solomon, entire book; I Corinthians 13, entire chapter; James 2:8; Titus 2:4; Colossians 3:19; Philippians 2:1-15; Ephesians 5:25-31; Galatians 5:13-15, 22-23; Romans Chapters 12 and 13; Galatians 3:14.

5.) These vows are made to each other, but also **to God**—both as a witness and to seek His enforcement for obvious or secret breaches of these vows.

   Malachi 2:14-16

6.) **To honor.** This is the pinnacle of our Covenant responsibility. The name, reputation, image, character, integrity, and overall person of the other party is promoted, enhanced, enlarged, improved, and praised whenever possible. To dishonor one's beloved or his or her reputation is the greatest dishonor one can inflict on one's Covenant. Honoring includes helping a person develop integrity, and helping them resolve other personal issues which might bring dishonor upon themselves. Honor speaks of the overall regard one has for another, of consistently choosing to view the other in the most positive possible light.

   Romans 12:10; I Corinthians 12:23-24, 13:5; I Peter 3:7; Proverbs 26:1, 31:10-31; I Thessalonians 4:4; Galatians 3:28; Hebrews 13:4.

7.) **To cherish.** To view as of highest value, to make the highest priority, to have the greatest regard for, to adore, to protect, to nurture, to defend, to revere, to esteem, to admire, to treasure, to prize—as well as to possess as one's own.

Song of Solomon; Proverbs 5:18-19; Ephesians 5:25-29.

8.) **To be faithful.** Faithfulness in Marriage is not merely physical—avoiding adultery. It is faithfulness to the principles of Covenant represented by these vows. The interests of one have become the interests of both. Faithfulness is the heartbeat of a Marriage. It is to become our guidance system, replacing feelings and desires with commitment. Faithfulness flows from our fixed and unchanging will to live for the best interests of the other party for a lifetime, regardless of any other consideration. This choice, and the unwavering commitment to live out this choice, are the essence of true love. True love for a lifetime is not a feeling, but a choice.

Ecclesiastes 5:4; Matthew 25:23; I Corinthians 4:2; Luke 16:10-13; Proverbs 28:20; Matthew 25:14-29; I Timothy 3:11; I Corinthians 13:13.

9.) **To be devoted.** This connotes loyalty, constancy, fidelity, commitment, dedication, and adherence to the other. There is also the sense of worshipping—not of the other person's humanity, but recognizing the Holy Spirit within our beloved.

I Corinthians 6:19; Romans 12:10; Luke 16:13.

10.) **Protection.** We stand against any physical risk to our beloved, but also against threats in the mental, emotional, and spiritual realm. These risks may arise from outside the relationship or from within either party. To protect includes speaking truth where there is lack of clarity, and searching out truth if it is not evident. It involves emotional support as well as defensive action. Spiritual protection involves seeking one's own spiritual growth, as well as promoting the spiritual growth of one's spouse; praying for one's partner, as well as defending against deception and deficient teaching of God's Word. Another risk we defend against is a lack of authenticity. Protection involves defense, but also teaching, mentoring, and leading by example. It is never the case that one party has everything in good order, while the other needs protecting. The injunction to protect, as in all things of Covenant, is a mutual obligation and must be mutually exercised.

Ezekiel 33:4, 6; Psalm 82:3; Hebrews 12:12; Galatians 6:1-2; II Corinthians 11:29; Hebrews 4:12; I Corinthians 13:7.

11.) **Provision.** This speaks to any material, emotional, or spiritual need which the other party can meet. This does not, however, mean the answer to every request is "yes." God loves us perfectly. Does He say yes to every request we make? He considers every request, and either gives us what we request or something better—what we actually need. God perfectly understands our real needs, in contrast to what we or others think is needed. Inherent in this commitment is the obligation for us to consider the deepest needs of the other party, beyond their simple requests, and to be wise and responsible. We do not have God's Omniscience, but we do have access to Him and can seek His wisdom. God on occasion will use us to point our spouse in a better direction. At the same time, Covenant is in every sense a blank check. It is the honor of each party to generously and graciously meet the true needs of their Covenant partner. This plan functions as intended only when this commitment is mutual, when both parties try to out-bless each other. Inherent in this obligation, we are to refrain from seeking frivolous or selfish things.

Proverbs 31:10-31; I Timothy 5:8; Luke 12:33; Proverbs 12:24; Matthew 5:42; James 2:14-26; Acts 4:35; I Timothy 3:5.

12.) **Trusting** in the other party, and **being trustworthy**. We pledge to trust this person, to believe their word and trust in their intentions unless we have unequivocal evidence to the contrary. If there are issues with honesty, we trust in the ultimate desire of the other to get things right. To believe in someone means we trust their ultimate desire for our best. This is why we marry someone in the first place, but both must prove worthy of this trust. Some character work may be necessary on this front—since we grew up in a culture that did not place high value on honesty and integrity. We should not take at face value the word of anyone who disparages our partner. Bring the matter before them and assume the best about them. In addition to accurate speech and overall honesty, another important mutual obligation is transparency, or full disclosure. We want to truly know each other, not know a false image crafted by concealing or exaggerating. Manipulation is not love.

I Timothy 3:11; Proverbs 31:11; Zechariah 8:16; Ephesians 4:25; Proverbs 22:21; Ephesians 4:15; Proverbs 8:7.

13.) **Perseverance**. Life is long and challenging. This concept is related to faithfulness, but highlights persistence, tenacity, and staying power. It is the distillation of our will, a refusal to yield in the face of difficulty or to back down when the price of faithfulness rises. We persevere in our commitment to love when circumstances or feelings change, or when we fend off attractions to other people and continue to act in loving ways when we are wounded, offended, or just weary.

Romans 5:4; II Peter 1:6; 2 Thessalonians 2:4, 3:5; Romans 5:4; James 1:3-4, 5:11; Hebrews 12:1.

14.) **Purity**. This is akin to the holiness of God—unstained, unpolluted. This is righteousness protected, honor lived out, the sum of virtues and the absence of vices. Purity is slowly approached as one matures spiritually, though never fully attained in this life. Inherent in this vow is our commitment to personal spiritual growth, and to the spiritual growth of the other party. We commit to display the best part of ourselves to the other, to give the best of ourselves, to spare them our shortcomings and character flaws when possible, as we deal with these things before God. The opposite of this would be acting as an agent of temptation, participating in the moral compromise of our partner.

II Corinthians 6:6; I Peter 3:2; Psalm 119:9; Proverbs 22:11; I Timothy 6:14; Ephesians 5:27; II Peter 3:14; I Peter 1:15-16; I Corinthians 6:19; Leviticus 20:26.

15.) **Honesty**. This is akin to trust/trustworthy, but has a larger meaning. Enlarging on the idea of transparency, this is a vow to reveal ourselves to the other party. This is an obligation to know ourselves and the other person better. The close proximity of Marriage is perfectly designed to reveal hidden parts of us to ourselves, and to the other person. Personal understanding grows most in an atmosphere of mutual honesty, love and acceptance. We are to correctly identify our own needs, feelings, and desires. For many this is a new frontier. A vital skill in Marriage is learning to ask for what we need from each other, at an appropriate time and in an appropriate way. First, we must determine what we really want or need, which may itself be a process. Then, we ask the one who loves us to meet our need or desire. But the next step is the absolute key: we have no right in the moment to insist on this outcome, or to manipulate in the face of reluctance. The key is to offer the other person the freedom to respond to our request in the moment, or to not do so. Even though the other person loves us and wants the best for us, still in this moment they may be unable to meet our needs for a variety of reasons. We must always be aware that the One who meets our needs is not our spouse, but God. Remember, sometimes God says "no" in the moment as well. Our spouse is not unlimited, as God is. Nor are we. We must make further allowances for each others limitations. The path to satisfaction in Marriage is graciously receiving whatever gift our spouse is capable of offering in the moment, even if it is "duly noted, I'll get back to you on that." If someone loves us, they will generally come back to this area, knowing that they can offer something that matters to us.

Honesty is vital if we are to really know each other—how we view things, how we feel about things, what we believe, what we really want. And beyond these, the areas we most often conceal—our deepest pain, our confusion, our uncertainty—in other words, our greatest vulnerabilities. These are things we should not reveal, except to someone who truly loves us and knows how to walk beside us in our imperfection. We often shield these things from our own view—thus, we never resolve these issues or grow beyond them. But our greatest progress often comes from doing just that. We must feel safe as we explore what is often the most dangerous neighborhood we will ever visit—the depths of our own mind and heart. We will never venture into these depths unless we are fully confident in the love of our God and our spouse, regardless of what we discover. Once there, in the midst of our own confusion, uncertainty, pain, fear, loneliness, and wounds, love and truth can set us free from all of these.

Ephesians 4:15, 25; Proverbs 4:24; James 5:12; Matthew 5:37; Colossians 3:9; I Corinthians 13:6.

16.) **Charity**. In contrast to mutual giving and receiving, the idea of charity involves asymmetric giving. Giving to one who cannot reciprocate, or offering grace and mercy to one who seems not to deserve it. The larger sense of charity is benevolence and good will, the desire for the best for another. We are to be conduits of God's grace to each other, offering kindness when condemnation or harshness would be an option. The sense of this would be to re-frame situations and wording to be as gracious as possible, while still being real and honest: *speaking the truth in love*. The essence of this vow is that our spouse may not at points be capable of reciprocating—the "worse, sicker, or poorer" part of the wedding vows. We are to be generous when it is only a one-sided transaction, and to do so indefinitely in the case of long-term illness or incapacity.

Luke 14:12-14; Colossians 3:12,19; I Peter 3:7; Romans 14:1, 15:7.

17.) Kindness. Kindness is a sincere concern for the feelings of the other party. This involves attention to feelings in situations where feelings might be overlooked.

Romans 11:22, 14:13-20; Colossians 3:12; II Corinthians 6:6; I Corinthians 13:4.

18.) **Patience**. We all have things we would like to see resolved yesterday, things that chafe more deeply because of repetition. We weary of recurring problems that seem easy to solve—to us. This vow acknowledges that life is long, some issues take time, and today's issue may not be as vital or important as we believe it to be. Though we are joined, the other person is on his or her own journey and brings a different set of tools and capacities to the table. People learn in different ways. It helps to understand what a bad day actually looks like. As a surgeon, seeing someone die from trauma, or cancer, or seeing someone's life change in permanent and significant ways helps put more minor irritants in perspective. Crises really do come in small, medium, and large. Small ones sometimes provoke large emotions, out of proportion with reality. We call these "trip wires" or "land mines." These merit attention, but should be dealt with as a separate issue. The common advice is, "Don't sweat the small stuff." Another lesson from surgery is understanding that the most constructive response to an actual crisis comes from a cool head and a steady hand. There is no place in life for losing control because we are "so upset." Patience is a vital form of self-control.

Ephesians 4:2; Romans 14:1-12; Colossians 3:12; I Corinthians 13:4.

19.) **Gentleness**. Akin to kindness, this has to do with more than emotions. This is the soft and careful way we are to deal with each other. This is about finding the most constructive way to say something, the least disruptive path to deal with an issue. It is about the pleasure and power of a soft touch. Subtlety can be more powerful than stridor. A gentle word can be most effective (Proverbs 15:1). As we observe people in Marriages trying to work through issues, it can be difficult to tell whether the two are friends or enemies. With a gentle approach, we know we are dealing with a friend.

Colossians 3:12; I Timothy 6:11; Galatians 5:23, 6:1; Philippians 4:5; Ephesians 4:2.

20.) **Self-control.** Akin to the several previous items, this is a summary word that speaks to being under the control of God's Spirit rather than carried away by ideas or passions that do harm. This reflects a guidance system based on truth and principle, rather than reaction and emotion. *God has not given us a spirit of fear, but of power, and love, and self-control* (2 Timothy 1:7). This involves our inner life of thought, emotion, values, priorities, attention, and will; and our outer life of attitude, word, and deed. It implies good moral choices, constructive relationship approaches, and constructive involvement in any situation. Inherent in this is an appropriate use of anger; avoiding collateral damage that occurs when anger spills beyond the specific, energetic, ultimately constructive and restorative response it is intended to be.

2 Peter 1:6; Galatians 5:23; Proverbs16:32, 25:28; I Corinthians 9:25; 2 Timothy 2:7.

21.) **To prefer you before all others, to forsake all others, to be yours and yours alone.** The other person is one's best friend. The two commit to remain best friends. No person and no consideration is more important than one's Marriage partner, except God Himself. Inasmuch as God is the author of Marriage, His interests coincide perfectly with living out the Covenant of Marriage faithfully and perfectly. In the plan of Covenant, God's will aligns perfectly with the deepest realities of two who are married, with their deepest desires, and with the best outcomes for Marriage and life. The two, face to face and side by side, face life as one, mirroring the Trinity—the Author of this relationship.

Proverbs 5:15-20; Malachi 2:15.

MY BELOVED AND MY MARRIAGE IN THE CENTER OF MY LIFE and THREE POWERS GIVEN TO US BY GOD

But seek first His kingdom and His righteousness, and all these things will be given you as well.
MATTHEW 6:33

As Holley and Mark were growing to adulthood it was generally assumed that a successful Marriage was more important than any other factor in building the best life. This cultural priority was reflected by the numbers— roughly five percent of marriages ended in divorce during our childhood. Not that previous generations did Marriage perfectly, but *the priority of Marriage and family* was vastly different based on the current percentage of people who marry—which is at the lowest level in the history of our nation, and the percentage of people who stay married, which has plummeted since 1960. Why did previous generations value Marriage more? Because it was assumed that the greatest rewards in life flow from our Marriage and family. Has this view also changed? What has taken the place of Marriage and family in our culture?

_____

_____

Marriage and family are central features in every culture through history. **What priority do you think God intends Marriage to have in our lives?** How important is Marriage? How important should one who chose to marry us be in our lives? He or she now occupies the center of our being. Our external lives are joined and merged. If our primary responsibility in life is to love this person as we love ourselves, what does this mean in practice? Other than a relationship with God, should spouse and family be first in my life? Should everything else in life play a secondary role? What does this mean in day-to-day life?

_____

_____

For where your treasure is, there your heart will be also.
LUKE 6:46

Covenant means we are to have **a level of commitment to our husband or wife that is stronger than any other human commitment.** Being faithful to our Covenant in every detail **ranks ahead of all other considerations.** We invest in the other **in ways that cultivates our own feelings.** We put away things that build or sustain contrary feelings. Of course, we honor, protect, provide for, and defend the other as we would ourselves. We are to devote ourselves to *becoming* the best mate through personal growth and transformation. Why is it imperative that Marriage have this priority?

_____

_____

What does this say about other important family relationships—ones we sometimes deem more important than our Marriage—such as children or parents?

_____

_____

…anyone who chooses to be a friend of the world becomes an enemy of God.
JAMES 4:4

What voices in our culture echo these priorities? In how many lives do we see these priorities lived out? What predictably happens if they are not? Our society teaches us much about living—beliefs, values, approaches, and many other things. Related to love and Marriage, **what priorities are commended by our culture?** These priorities do not come to us in the form of an extensive explanation. Instead, we hear sound-bites and see advertisements for certain behaviors—the ones that really make life worth living. Or that make us *matter* in our culture—*having* this…*doing* that…*being* this or that. **Our significance is reduced to in-the-moment impressions instead of flowing from a relationship wisely built over a lifetime.** Feedback on FaceBook replaces the affirmation of a close friend. One night stands replace marital intimacy. Education is far more important than family. We break up with the love of our life to pursue that dream job. Marriage and family are discarded in favor of…what? What is more valuable in the long run? We seem convinced that these new values are leading us toward a better, brighter, more educated, more scientifically based and technologically sophisticated future. But, look around. Is this a new era of happiness and satisfaction? Is total commitment really the path to bondage? Or is it the doorway to the best Marriage?

_____

_____

Do *you* believe this level of commitment is the *key* to the best Marriage?

_____

_____

If you are not fully confident of this at the moment, do you think it is *possible* that this is true—that this *is* God's plan and that He *just might* know what He is talking about?

We often absorb cultural assumptions without considering them, or understanding where these thoughts lead, or realizing they are becoming part of our personal guidance system. It seems that these are what "everyone knows." As we embrace and live out some of our current cultural ideas, though, we replicate the moral life of ancient Rome. Does this move us forward? We eagerly look for the next invention or discovery to provide the lives we long for because…why? Because we are not living that life now? More of the same is likely to produce more of what? Relationships—specifically learning the high-level relationship skills needed to build and maintain quality relationships—have gone missing in many lives.

Despite whatever has shifted, one thing remains the same: we are created for relationship. **We need love like we need air and water.** How many of us are starving—for love? What is the answer here? Let us look closer at **what guides our behavior.** Why do we do what we do? It all comes down to **our beliefs.** And all our beliefs come down to **choices we have made.** A better relationship, or better life overall comes down to *shifting our beliefs* **into accord with truth.** Therefore, we must review and revise *previous choices* based on *new information.* This process is one of the centerpieces of God's Covenant plan. Let's start by looking at a simple question.

What are people trained to pursue **instead of** key relationships? Money, fame, power, popularity, status, or simply self-expression and self-interest. The goal is to be **better than**…to rise above others by some measure. **Anything that gives us an advantage over others will do.** Cyberspace is the new playground and the newest app makes one the coolest kid. But climbing over others is not the same as relating to others. Nothing can replace a personal conversation—reading expression and tone of voice. Or learning to discern unspoken motives. In other words, truly getting to know the one with whom you communicate. Nothing can replace meeting needs and blessing others. Some needs can only be met through deep and transparent relationships. While success in any realm is not inherently a bad thing, if we sacrifice deep relationships to pursue success we lose in the end. And if we compromise our character and integrity in the process these losses are compounded.

What do you **treasure most** in your life?

God has placed within us three powers, or capabilities. These powers enable us to hear His truth and His directives. Then to live these out, faithfully obeying our Lord in all of life. But these same powers can be misdirected, leading us into the weeds or off a cliff. How? By choosing to *embrace as truth* things that *are not true,* then **implementing these things in our lives.** How, then, can we know what is actually true? This is one of the most important questions in all of life. God has provided the answer to this vital question. And created within us the power to live these truths when we find them.

THE THREE POWERS GIVEN TO US BY GOD

These powers are among the most powerful tools we have for life-building and life-change. But we may not be aware these powers even exist, or how powerful they are—much less how to use them. These are the powers of **Assent and Dissent, Attention,** and **Intention.** Basically, these represent our power to: 1.) decide whether *we believe an idea is true or false;* 2.) decide *how important this idea is to us*; and 3.) decide *what, if anything, we are going to do about it.* In each of these things our decisions are final. No one can force us to believe something, or value something, or do something if we choose not to…if we are willing to endure the consequences. Our Creator respects the power to choose that He placed within us. We get to choose what we believe about Him, how much we value Him, and what we do in response to Him and His love. Of course, these decisions have consequences…

When the Spirit of Truth comes He will guide you into all truth.
JOHN 16:13

Your will know the truth and the truth will set you free…
JOHN 8:32

Truthful words stand the test of time.
PROVERBS 12:19

THE POWER OF ASSENT AND DISSENT

We encounter many ideas every day. Each of us is given **the power to decide** which ones **are true** and which **are not.** Understand, our decision **does not establish** that something is **actually true**—only that **we believe it to be true.** People make such decisions every day—about what to buy or wear, and about more important life issues. Oddly, every **big, life-directing question** in life is subject to debate. From the existence of God to the origins of life and humanity, to the meaning of life and what happens next—for each question there are a *number of possible answers*, and we make **our choice.** Two people can decide conflicting ideas are true. Both could not be. Perhaps neither is actually true. Have you ever been convinced of something, only to find later that it was anything but true? How much confidence should we have in our own ability to choose what is *actually true* for these most-important, life-directing questions?

_____

_____

_____

THE IMPACT OF AFFIRMED IDEAS

It is important to understand *what else* happens when we decide an idea is true—especially **a significant, life-directing idea.** For, instance, you conclude that your path to the best life is to become rich or famous, or to meet the expectations of your peer group or your family, or whatever. An embraced idea *shifts our viewpoints.* This idea becomes *something we are sure of about life.* Our minds do not like conflicting ideas, so we adjust other viewpoints into harmony with this new one. We embrace similar ideas more easily, and may stop taking opposing views seriously. This idea **becomes part of our sense of reality**, and may become **part of our guidance system** (if it is a "what I should do" idea). Or, it can form **part of our character** (if it is a "how I should be" idea). If someone "seems different"—for instance, when he or she comes home from college for the first time—you are seeing these processes at work.

Since an embraced idea now represents reality to us, people holding different ideas do not just have a different opinion. *They are wrong.* If we believe someone is completely misguided on an important issue, how do we view this person? Our reaction is magnified by **the way an embraced idea changes our feelings.** We feel good about our accepted ideas and those who share them. We feel *negative feelings* toward conflicting views and the misguided souls who embrace them. **Some ideas become part of our internal legal system as well.** If a person's view threatens a cherished pillar of our belief system, this violation of reality itself merits condemnation or even punishment. If you are not clear about the power of these effects, look at the cultural and political debates in our society. Disagreements are no surprise, but the level of contempt and hatred displayed toward those with different political views is shocking. We see this same level of contempt in many public and academic references to Christian beliefs. All of this illustrates the power of affirming a belief. Have you ever had this kind of surprisingly negative response from someone?_____

We point out extremes to illustrate this reality. Most situations are not so visible or dramatic—but they exist. Affirmed beliefs exert an impact on minds, hearts, and relationships. Do you believe **feelings are impacted by what we believe?** What if you **believe I stole your wallet?** How will you feel toward me the next time you see me? But, what if you find your misplaced wallet? How do you feel toward me then? One cannot say, "I am going to feel this way instead of that way." Our hearts do not work that way. If feelings are based on a belief that is not true, though, how **could we change how we feel?**

_____

_____

Actual truth is a statement of reality. God's **moral truth** is a statement about **inevitable consequences.** Therefore, a life based on **actual truth** *is in harmony with reality,* and is filled with *good consequences and internal experiences.* What about lies and deception? Lives based on these are an accumulation of bad consequences and negative experiences. How important is it **to identify and affirm actual truth** and brand lies for what they are, versus embracing lies and rejecting truth? How can this be done?

_____

_____

We do not fix what is not broken. But what if **an emotion causes recurring problems**, or one is **devoted to an inappropriate goal**? What if **conflicting beliefs create division** in a Marriage? The couple can simply try to avoid these trouble spots. They can learn to fight less destructively, but there is a more successful approach. That is, for each to examine *the ideas and viewpoints that play a role in the conflict.* Perhaps some things we accepted as true at one point are not in fact true. How do we know this? We can be confident an idea is not true if it **opposes God's Word**. Do you believe this? Why or why not?

_____

_____

Earlier, I mentioned that Holley and I have shifted discussions of our different agendas—from trying to be right to trying to *get it right*. What if *getting it right* goes deeper than our belief about who should empty the dishwasher? What if **getting it right means looking at the ideas** upon which our viewpoints or feelings are based? These ideas may be right, or might be a deception we embraced without realizing it. What if *getting it right* means **getting our ideas in line with God's Word**? Would it be better to just get the dishwasher emptied, or better to weed out an idea that is the enemy of our souls and our relationship? Instead of adversaries with competing views and agendas, what if **we become allies in a search for the truth about every aspect of life**? What kind of relationship does this build? How does this search for truth fit into your relationship?

_____

_____

What is the difference between merely hearing these ideas and embracing them?

_____

_____

_____

_____

…fix your thoughts on Jesus…
Hebrews 3:1

…whatever is true, whatever is noble, whatever is right, whatever is pure, whatever is lovely, whatever is admirable—if anything is excellent or praiseworthy, think about such things.
Philippians 4:8

THE POWER OF ATTENTION

Hold your hand a foot in front of your face with your fingers spread apart. First, focus on what is beyond your hand. Do you see your fingers clearly? Now, focus on your fingers. Does the background blur? **You just used your power of attention.** We can focus on only one thing, or perhaps a few things at any one time. **We get to choose what we focus upon.** Do you realize the significance of this ability? We can focus on the pain of the sprain, or on the importance of the game and the key role we are called on to play. We can focus on a loss and the role another played, or we can focus on God as our true source for provision and the lesson He may want to teach us through this adversity. We can focus on words that question the character of a friend, or trust in our friend until we have conclusive evidence. What difference does it make whether we focus on one thing or the other?

We use this power to **weigh the relative importance** of things we view as true. These decisions form our *value system* and our *priorities*. Is a balanced family budget more important, or impressing our friends with clothing or trips? Beyond these particulars **we decide on life goals** from among many contenders. In the end, what will be most important for us to do, or be? We make choices about all these things and many more.

We all have **a ruler we use to measure the relative worth of things**. This measuring scale is also based on ideas we have embraced as true. Therefore, our values may include incorrect or deceptive ideas. Are we climbing a ladder leaning against the wrong wall? **For this power we also need to seek actual truth, and base our priorities and goals upon it.** Even true and virtuous things must be put in proper order. The goal is a properly directed, properly balanced life. Single life is complex; married life far more so, and complexity multiplies when we add children to the mix. How many ways do you use this power in your life now?

Set your minds on things above, not on earthly things.
COLOSSIANS 3:2

We can **focus only on the physical world**—much like looking at our fingers in the exercise above, and not see beyond these into the spiritual realm. If we do, though, we miss the larger context of our actions or circumstances. It is remarkably helpful to **return our focus to the spiritual realm on a very regular basis.** We can ignore this realm, or we can build our viewpoints, priorities, character, and life upon its truths, and walk faithfully hand in hand with the Author of these truths. **Everything about Covenant is a spiritual truth.** We must seek the truth about our Marriage in this realm. One such truth is the priority of our partner and relationship. Do you see the importance of using this power to put our spouse and our Marriage in their proper position in life? This is essential if we are to faithfully live out our Covenant. How aware are you of the spiritual realm on a typical day?

He who is faithful with little is faithful with much.
LUKE 16:10

Now that you have purified yourselves by obeying the truth so that you have sincere love for each other, love each other fervently from the heart.
I Peter 1:22

…these are in conflict with each other, so that you are not to do whatever you want.
Galatians 5:17

THE POWER OF INTENTION

This power accomplishes the things we deem truly important. It is the force which translates good intentions into effective, completed *actions*. **In a world full of things we could do, this part of us determines what gets done.** Weakness of this power creates problems with follow-through. If this power is underdeveloped we remain full of good intentions—could have, should have, would have…but didn't. No one can *make us* do something we absolutely refuse to do. Nor can any obstacle stand in our way if we are absolutely determined to accomplish something. When have you been *absolutely determined* to do something?

This power **ensures love in action.** Or, if not used, the lack thereof. It ensures that we **fulfill responsibilities,** or we can fail to do so. We can **build our new self,** or we can remain immature and undeveloped. We can **revise our guidance system,** or continue to be guided by ideas that are dysfunctional and out-of-date. Like any ability, **this power can be strengthened** by making a point of following through with small daily tasks. Once we are consistent with these we can think about larger-scale uses of this power. **It is vital for us to grasp the importance of being faithful in all things**—big things and small things, words and actions. And equally vital that we **unleash the full power of our intention to live out these priorities.** The way we use this power directly impacts the trust and respect others have for us, and determines the growth of our character. How do you *build your resolve* to be faithful?

The first thing that impressed me about Holley's character was her follow-through. Whatever she said she would do, she did. She called when she said she would, and showed up when she said she would. I found I could trust her words. I learned she would honor her commitments. What impact do you think this had on our relationship?

A pitfall in close relationships is viewing **a recurring lack of follow-through** as an isolated issue. This involves more than simply *choosing not to do something.* We are wise to *understand the foundation required for proper use of this power.* Correct beliefs, priorities, and values must be in place for one to follow through consistently. If this foundation is not in place, *applying pressure* to our spouse may work for some issues, but will lead to escalating frustration and conflict overall. This is a time to look deeper into ourselves. When did this pattern begin, and why? What ideas guided the decision *not to do* what the person *knew he or she should do*? And, why did this pattern become a way of life? What idea or emotion drove this? We must understand the beliefs in play, and seek change at this level. If this is done, better follow-through will be one of many benefits. Does this different approach make sense to you? Why or why not?

_____

_____

OUR THREE POWERS ARE THE BATTLEFIELD IN A SPIRITUAL WAR

Why are there so many **false and deceptive ideas** in our world, and **why** do so many **agree with them and implement them**? *We are in a spiritual war.* Our minds, hearts, and wills are the battlefield in that war. The weapons on one side are truth and love, on the *other* lies, deception, and all the destructive things people inflict on one another. It is crucial to understand that each exercise of these powers involves a decision about what we decide is true and what is not. Therefore, each decision we make at this level influences the course of our life. These three powers play the central role in building our characters, and *directing the course* of our lives and marriages. If this is true, where do you think the enemies of God might focus their attention to do the most damage? Might they sell us lies and deceptions that *corrupt our guidance system,* and *build dysfunction into our character*? We are continually presented with false ideas packaged as the path to our best life; we are beset with distractions and overloaded with things that *divert us from pursuing the best things.* We are lulled, discouraged, or intimidated into inactivity, **instead of aggressively building our Marriages and our lives.** The *last* thing our enemy wants to see are wonderful, loving, fruitful Marriages, for this is proof that his lies are *in fact lies.* In the face of this kind of evidence it is much harder for him to persuade people to embrace his lies as truth, and embrace paths that damage and destroy.

Are you building a Marriage that worries our enemy?

_____

_____

_____

_____

LESSON SIX

SEEKING PERFECTION and ABSOLUTE TRUTH IN OUR MORAL UNIVERSE

Covenant is an all-in kind of thing. We offer our lives to each other with nothing held back. We accept the other into the center of our lives without reservation. We accept and fully embrace God's plan for Marriage. And we vow to carry out God's plan in its entirety, and in every detail. We vow to love another perfectly in mind, heart, word, and deed, and to faithfully follow through with every responsibility that is part of Covenant.

> *"This is now bone of my bones and flesh of my flesh;...That is why a man leaves his father and mother and is united to his wife, and they become one flesh.*
> Genesis 2:23, 24

Then, we wake up the next morning, the first day of the rest of our life together, and… enjoy the amazing blessings of our life together. We stay positive, keep building, and integrate piece after piece of our lives within our new relationship. For quite awhile we are in the grip of the most intense feelings we have ever had. We continue to delight in finding ways to express our love. We clearly get along well—*though not perfectly.* We move down the merge lane into our new married life and settle into a new routine. Our routine is great in many ways, *but not perfect.* Nor do we expect it to be. What, though, do we expect it to be? Whatever we expect, we soon find there are a few rough edges we did not see coming. The cute, charming things we admired at a distance may become annoying up close on a daily basis. The free spirit that delighted us as it flittered here and there may become the absent-minded person who forgets to do important things. The "his own person," hard-charging, "do it his way" exciting playmate may become the stubborn guy who does not listen well, or at all. It's still good, but things are starting to cool in paradise. Do we ignore the rough edges? Do we say something? Are we not willing to settle for…? Or do we settle for…? Do we not sweat the small stuff? Is this small stuff, or…? Do I have a right to…? Does he or she have any right to…?

What happens next is remarkably important. The pattern the two build to respond to these challenges does much to determine the quality of the Marriage. What did you do at this point in your Marriage?

_____

_____

...in the image of God He created them; male and female He created them...
God saw all that He had made, and it was very good.
GENESIS 1:27,31

Two build a great love **by just being themselves**—at *the safe distance of single-hood.* But when *impressive and interesting* turns into completely interrelated and interdependent, the equation changes. *The stakes get higher to make sure that...***what?** That we get enough of **our way** to feel like life is on the right track? That **loving actions keep flowing our way,** and fuel more loving feelings to keep this thing alive? Is **more leverage** the answer, along with a sweet smile? God has a different plan.

"For I know the plans I have for you," declares the Lord, "plans to prosper
you and not to harm you, plans to give you hope and a future."
JEREMIAH 29:11

The path of Covenant is simply stated. Make loving your Covenant partner your highest priority, make faithfulness to your Covenant your highest priority, and define love as God does. This is not about "because God says so," but *in order to build the best Marriage—and the best you.* The blessings that flow from this life cannot be overstated, but we cannot see *the life this path will produce* on the front end. If we could, that would be sufficient motivation to follow God's plan with every fiber of our being. But we cannot. **We need other motivation to make a new set of choices.** We need to see that God has a plan, one God said is "very good." We need to embrace His plan as our own. Then, as the shoe says, "Just do it." Are you embracing God's plan as your own? Why or why not?

_____

_____

Be perfect, therefore, as your heavenly father is perfect.
MATTHEW 5:48

Be perfect. Try your best. *Try harder...*no, **harder**! The word perfection can be a lightning rod. Some have been badly burned by the *human* view of this concept. Someone else required perfection of us...or we couldn't be loved. We failed, and were not loved. So we set out to prove ourselves. We required perfection of ourselves...and failed, but nevertheless became a *perfectionist.* How did this plan work? It was ultimately frustrating, painful, even shameful. Why? We followed the plan of the world, in our own strength, doing what we thought would work. With this background, how do we respond when God lays expectations on us? But is God's plan the same as the one we have already disproven? God first transforms us, then invites us to learn to live authentically—to *reflect Him and His love* in our marriage. Isn't it easier to be who we are than to act like anything else? What kind of relationship do you have with the word "perfection"?

———————————————————————————————————————

———————————————————————————————————————

> *Anyone who loves me will obey my teaching. My Father will love them,*
> *and We will come to them and make Our home with them.*
> JOHN 14:23

God has built many motivations into Covenant to point us toward His path and *reward us for walking this path*. First, **we love each other and our hearts are on fire for the other,** at least some of the time. Loving actions makes perfect sense to a *heart full of love*. But we are not *always* carried along by these feelings. What happens in those moments when loving actions and attitudes do not make sense to us? What happens when other priorities crowd into minds, hearts, and circumstances, and lead us in another direction?

GOD'S MOTIVATIONAL SYSTEM WITHIN COVENANT

How does God motivate us to follow His plan if we do not feel like *doing loving things*?

1.) **Our love.** We chose to marry each other because we are in love. The best heart experience we will ever have is feeling, receiving, and expressing love. We want to love our husband or wife more, or *want* to want to love them more. We want our love to last, to become happily-ever-after. This is one of our strongest human drives.

2.) **Positive reinforcement/building good consequences.** What happens when we build our relationship, draw closer together, and develop a more intimate, transparent, supportive and caring relationship? Every move in this direction builds an experience worth having. We feel it. These are good times; we want more of them.

3.) **Our commitment.** We *vowed* to love each other in every way.

4.) **The underlying reality of Covenant.** Consistent love-in-action makes perfect sense, for it perfectly reflects every reality of Covenant. Love is authentic; acting in unloving ways *does not* make any sense if we grasp this reality.

5.) **The teaching of Scripture.** God's overall directive is clearly stated: unending, uncompromising, unwavering love toward each other. God then defines many details about love through injunctions and examples in Scripture.

6.) **The historic institution of Marriage.** Many cultural expectations surround Marriage among Christians, which reflect the responsibilities inherent in this relationship. Until recently, this is what "everyone knew" about Marriage and how to conduct one. How has a commitment-laden institution like Marriage been so durable over millennia? Because **many practices of Marriage reflect the reality of Marriage**, and are not affected by other cultural beliefs. This durability reflects the many vital roles played by Marriage and family in individual lives, as well as in cultures. *The historic vows of Marriage cited earlier were drawn from many cultures over many centuries.* The durability and consistency of these vows bear testimony to the sameness of Marriage across many centuries in the lives of those who know God. Marriage is a very specific thing, regardless of what we try to make it. What does it mean to *seek* to love perfectly?

_____

_____

7.) We live in a universe that is not just physical—matter, energy, chemistry, and physics. It is also moral. **God created a system of cause and effect in our universe that mirrors the moral teaching of Scripture.** Every action, word, attitude, and thought results in a series of consequences. Some consequences, like a person's reaction, may occur in the moment. Other consequences may be delayed hours or decades, but they will occur. We *can* choose our actions or words, but we cannot choose their consequences. This realm is reserved for God.

ABSOLUTE TRUTH IN OUR MORAL UNIVERSE

Do not be deceived. God cannot be mocked. A man reaps what he sows.
GALATIANS 6:7

Consequences do not impact only their author; they also impact others. Imagine throwing a rock in a pond. We see ripples spreading in every direction. Consequences are like this. Now, imagine people surrounding a pond, all throwing rock after rock into the water. Consequences flow outward in all directions in a growing group of waves which wash over everyone on shore. **This is our world—awash in consequences.** This is the reason many people have terrible life circumstances through no fault of their own. Consequences may be positive or negative. Fortunately, good things also have broad impact. But our world, caught up in *rebellion against God*, is awash in the consequences of the cumulative sins of humanity. These consequences inevitably impact our marriages. How have the consequences of another's actions deeply impacted you?

_____

_____

They sow the wind, and they shall reap the whirlwind...
HOSEA 8:7

Many people do not understand the relationship between actions and consequences. This is part of the spiritual dimension of life—one of the ways in which the unseen spiritual universe impacts the universe we can see. Many today believe that bad life outcomes are all about luck or victimhood. They do not see the role played by cause and effect. Since consequences may be long delayed, we may not make the connection between today's job loss and previous lapses of integrity. Or, connect a damaged or lost relationship with a pattern of unloving actions. The sound-bite is "the two just fell out of love." Did choices—words, actions, and attitudes—play any role? Many people are more the author of their circumstances than they realize. Pray that God's Word and His Spirit will search our heart, and show us our role in our current problems. Record what He shows you.

_____

_____

Love does no wrong to others, so love fulfills the requirements of God's law.
ROMANS 13:10

Love does not rejoice in evil, but rejoices in the truth.
I CORINTHIANS 13:6

Everyone did what was right in his own eyes...
JUDGES 21:25 (NASB)

There is a way that appears to be right, but in the end it leads to death.
PROVERBS 16:25

...God's kindness is intended to lead you to repentance...
ROMANS 2:4

LOVE VS. CONSEQUENCES

People in our day assume they are *free to do and speak as they want*—in fact, people have a self-proclaimed right to do so. In their minds, others are supposed to not only receive the damage caused by their behaviors, words, attitudes, and priorities, but *embrace and even celebrate them for "being themselves."* This person believes true **love** means **fully accepting them as they are, period.** Many think they can engage in immorality and rebellion without consequence. If no one sees or knows, who cares? And isn't right and wrong a personal matter, different for each person? **Before all consequences have occurred, one can believe these things based on what has happened to this point.** But because of the moral nature of our universe—and the God who watches over it—**a high price is always paid for moral breaches. There are no exceptions.** God's love, forgiveness, and grace do not change the number on the price tag of temporal consequences—loss of opportunities, credit, friends, job, family relationships, reputation, or a Marriage. Genuine repentance may lead to a second chance, or not. David repented of adultery with Bathsheba and was forgiven by God. But a child died, and from this point David's family and kingdom were filled with strife. **God is serious about motivating us to stop damaging ourselves and others.** Consequences are a powerful tool to reinforce His intent—if we understand them. Have your words or actions ever had far more serious consequences than you expected?

_____

_____

_____

_____

HARNESSING THE POWER OF GOOD CONSEQUENCES

Think for a moment how it would be if you had an unending series of good consequences—in your life and in your Marriage. Instead of *in-the-moment things*, it helps if we think of things we do as *planting seeds*. Imagine you are carrying two bags slung across your shoulder. One bag is labeled "good seeds" and the other "weeds and thorns." No matter the circumstances, if you are trying to grow something worthwhile in your field, which bag will you reach into? Which seeds would you toss into your field? Is there *any reason* you would voluntarily toss weeds and thorns into the middle of your precious crops—things you might never be rid of once they start growing? Regardless of how you feel in the moment, **why make a much larger headache for yourself in the future?** What are these good seeds? Loving actions. These always yield good consequences now and in the future. Have you ever experienced far more positive consequences from an action than you expected? Why?

_____

_____

OUR AFFIRMED TRUTHS VS. ACTUAL TRUTH

You may have already noticed a key insight. We spoke of our power to *determine what we believe to be true*. We noted that **our decision that something is true** does not mean that it **is true.** That is a completely different question. Part of being human is embracing some ideas about self and life that are not true. **A consistent theme in this study is the need to find actual truth.** If we base our lives on real truth, relationship grows, we thrive, and good consequences abound. If, however, we embrace and live out ideas that are not true *we head in the wrong direction*—relationships are damaged, our lives become more challenged and conflicted, and we unleash negative consequences. Every life is a mixture of getting some things right and others wrong. The plan of God, and the theme of this study, is **shifting our embraced ideas** from **think it is true to know it is true.** However, since any individual or group is apt to get a thing wrong, *how can we know what is* **actually true**? Is this even possible? What is *your* bottom-line source for truth, that trumps all others?

_____

_____

All Scripture is inspired by God and profitable for teaching,
for reproof, for correction, and for training in righteousness.
II Timothy 3:16 (NASB)

Sanctify them by the truth; Your Word is truth.
John 17:17

WHERE DO WE FIND ACTUAL TRUTH?

I ran head-on into this question as I was considering becoming a Christian. I went to a very liberal university, so I already had a strong bias against the Scriptures being the entire, intact, literal words of God. Instead, I viewed Scripture as a collection of writings expressing the religious aspirations of people through the ages. I faced a simple question. I was willing to bow my knee before God (if there was one) but not to human religion or human writings. So, *what was I reading* as I read the Scriptures? Do they speak reliably about God? Should I do what they say? Are these the very words of God to me? Or, are these human myths *edited to be more impressive*—as if prophesy had been fulfilled, or as if Jesus was God? Would I be a fool to follow these words?

While I was considering these questions, Josh McDowell came to our medical school to do a week-long seminar. He presented evidence for several key Christian beliefs. One belief was the nature of the Scriptures. We cannot recount that evidence here (though I strongly recommend reviewing it in his book, *Evidence that Demands a Verdict* [5]). There is compelling evidence that the Scriptures have been maintained in essentially word-for-word original form for thousands of years. This is utterly unique, *unlike any other writing from the ancient world.* A vast number of archeological discoveries corroborate Scriptural accounts. Opinions and interpretations of individual archeologists may differ from Scripture, but there are *no actual findings with uncontested dates which do so.*

The moral instructions in Scripture are clear, consistent, and coherent across the writings of many human contributors. All of these writings point to Christ. But for me, what authenticated their Divine source was *fulfilled prophesy.* There are hundreds of very specific predictions in Scripture. There is compelling evidence that most of these were written well before the events in question. In every case history shows these predictions to be precisely accurate. Nothing like this exists anywhere else in human literature or experience. **This makes the Scriptures a source of truth not subject to human imperfection, a source upon which I can base my life with 100% confidence.** I embraced this position over forty years ago, and have had no reason to amend this decision. God has proven Himself utterly trustworthy not only in theory but in practice across all of life.

Have you searched these truths out for yourself?

BUILDING A FOUNDATION OF ACTUAL TRUTH FOR OUR LIFE

If embracing actual truth is so important, if this is *the thing needed* to properly direct our lives, **how do we build this foundation**? Obviously, we need to become very familiar with the source of this truth, the Scriptures. This means *reading and studying the entirety of God's Word.* We must spend considerable time ingesting the Word on a regular basis. We must not only *know* what God says, we must apply His truths to the world in which we live, and to our lives. This means we must meditate on key truths—important passages and Scriptures. It helps to memorize those most needed for our life. What? How could God's plan take *this much time and effort*? Well, how much time do people devote to online education for career advancement, or for training in any other realm? How much time are we spending now in the world's training process of media and culture each day? If we spent even a fraction of the time the average person spends each day exposing themselves to media and other sources of mis-education, we could master the basics of God's Word in a couple of years. In another year or so we could have applied the basic truths of His Word to the major questions of life. Before long, we would have a deep understanding of the heart and mind of God. This understanding, and our faithfulness, allow us to walk with Him in an intimate relationship. We cover this process in detail in the *The New Covenant* by this author. Basically, **we must fully embrace His truth**—actual truth—as our truth and live it out.

I am very successful in many ways. I have confidence in my own perceptions and opinions. I am not easily swayed by other's opinions. Except from one source. **If God's opinion is different from mine, He is right and I am wrong. Period.** I have found no exception to this in over forty years in hundreds of situations. God wants to teach us truth in every realm of life. Why? Because He loves us and wants the best for us. It just so happens that **a life based on actual truth is better than any other.** None of us ever gets there completely in this life, but moving in that direction is worth any effort. This is especially true regarding our Marriage. How important is finding and applying *actual truth* in your life?

Sanctify them by the truth; Your word is truth.
JOHN 17:17

Lord, to whom shall we go? You have the words of eternal life.
JOHN 6:68

God "will repay each person according to what they have done."
ROMANS 2:6

IT'S THE LITTLE THINGS...

Every move we make in relationship either builds or tears down. There is literally *nothing* we do that does not matter. Envision a path in front of you. You can turn right—build—or left, and un-build. You can only move in one direction at a time, but can change directions as often as you like. It is helpful to think of *following God's plan* as **a path we travel.** We may commit to following God's plan, to walk in one direction, to love consistently. But, if we make this commitment we must **consistently live it out** by making many decisions on a daily basis. This can be challenging. But, what would our Marriage be like if we only did things that build?

_____

_____

_____

WHAT WOULD IT BE LIKE...

Think for a moment about your Marriage. What would it be like if there were no pointless arguments or fights to see who gets their way; no manipulation or words said just to wound; no secrets, put-downs, or bringing up the past; no sharing of your faults and failings with others, and no need to hide behind an image? **What if there was no need to be anything but yourself?** What would it be like to be supported, to have your needs recognized and met, to be treated with kindness and respect—always? And what would it be like for your husband or wife to always receive such treatment from you? What would it be like for your heart to soar whenever you see your husband or wife? For your husband or wife to be welcomed in every part of your life? To really miss your spouse whenever he or she is not around? To know you will be more in love with this person next year than you are now? Does this describe your Marriage? If not, do you believe God's plan can produce such a relationship if you both follow His plan?

_____

_____

THE TRUTH ABOUT TRUE LOVE

God wants to open our eyes to some realities about true love. Love is not *just* about feelings. **True love is about commitment and action.** True love is about *making the other first in our life, and aligning the rest of our priorities accordingly.* **Covenant is designed to be an all-in thing on the part of both parties**—two people fully committed to each other, **who learn to build together** everything necessary for Marriage and family—including *themselves.* This is how love continues to grow for a lifetime. This is God's plan, but Marriages reflect this plan to varying degrees. Is true love something we find, or build? Explain:

_____

_____

Why do we emphasize all of this? We mentioned early on that Covenant informs us about not only *what we do*, but *why we do these things*. And not only this, but **how we become able to do them**. I do not know about you, but I am not very good at "because I said so." At this point in life, if someone cannot give me a good reason I assume they do not have one. **The exception is God, who may not share His reasons.** "Because I said so" is sufficient from Him. But if He opens His reasoning to us, I find **I have a much easier time following His lead.** Especially when His reasoning is about a massive and multifaceted plan that I need to embrace wholeheartedly. **In Covenant we have found this understanding.**

> *Where there is no vision (or revelation), the people are unrestrained…*
> PROVERBS 29:18 (NASB)[5]

What is your vision for your Marriage?

_____

_____

_____

_____

_____

_____

A VISION FOR OUR MARRIAGE

If we are to follow God's plan, **God must first give us a vision for our Marriage**. We need a picture of how something is supposed to look. A blueprint to build a house. Or a young person watching a professional sport, artistic performance, or intellectual pursuit—and wanting this to be *their life*. First, we embrace the vision; then, we go about building it. What if you could unroll a blueprint for everything your Marriage might become according to God's plan? You really like what you see, and you see what is necessary to get there. *Would you be more inclined to do whatever it takes to build this Marriage?* **In our culture we see fewer and fewer great marriages.** Many people never see one up close, much less develop a clear picture of how such a Marriage is built.

> *…put off your old self..to be made new in the attitude of your minds; and to put on the new self…*
> EPHESIANS 4:22-24

If we set our wills to follow God's plan; if we *learn* all we can about love and *follow through* in every way we can **we will still have an internal conflict**. We will find *we cannot do and be these things as consistently as we hope*. As Paul says in Romans 7:15, "For what I want to do I do not do, but what I hate, I do." He is speaking of the challenge of obeying God in a larger sense, but this also applies in Marriage. What is going on? Something within us needs to be transformed. Our identity has already been transformed, so what else needs to change? **Our intention to authentically live out our new identity and our Covenant will be**

opposed by parts of our own guidance system—by ideas embraced before we were Married. This remains our guidance system unless we take specific steps to revise it.

Love does not delight in evil but rejoices with the truth.
It always protects, always trusts, always hopes, always perseveres.
I Corinthians 13:6-7

Submit to one another out of reverence for Christ.
Ephesians 5:21

Husbands, love your wives, just as Christ loved the church and gave Himself up for her...
Ephesians 5:25

He who loves his wife loves himself.
Ephesians 5:28

Wives, submit to your husband as you do to the Lord...
Ephesians 5:22

The wife must respect her husband.
Ephesians 5:33

In the next lesson we will learn more about our guidance system, and why so much *mis-information* is being sold to humanity as truth. To do this, we will pay a visit to the home of a married couple—the first married couple. Based on what we learn, we will see *how our guidance system can be fixed:* **we must become affixed** to *actual truth*. Then we will see what kind of relationship is produced if our guidance system is directed by God instead of the world around us.

LESSON SEVEN

DEALING WITH IMPERFECTION and THE GARDEN OF EDEN: ADAM AND EVE, TRUTH AND DECEPTION

He who is faithful in a very little thing is faithful also in much; and he who is unrighteous in a very little thing is also unrighteous in much.
LUKE 16:10

Jesus replied, "Rather, how blessed are those who hear and obey God's word."
LUKE 11:28

THE CENTERPIECE OF COVENANT IS FAITHFULNESS.

This word encompasses **everything we are to do and be, and everything within us**—our thoughts, feelings, intentions, motives, goals, and priorities. Christians want more faith, but what is faith? If we are *full of faith*, are we not faith-full…or faithful? Faith is not just a state of mind or heart. Faith is a transformed life that is expressed in acts of obedience. God desires that faithfulness become ***the one word which best describes our character***—the way we approach life and relationship overall, and in each detail. The point is to *build relationship and build our capacity to love*. Faithfulness is the path that leads to this destination. **Ideals are laid before us in Marriage**. The issue then comes down to our choices. We may embrace these ideals and devote our lives to pursuing them, choose bits and pieces, or keep doing life our way. What are your thoughts on faithfulness?

_____

_____

FAITHFULNESS IS BOTH A DECISION AND A PROCESS

Let's suppose you really want to follow God and commit yourself to Him and His plan. You probably have a really good relationship with a few rough edges. **Most of us want to focus on the positive, build on the good things, and pretty much get past any rough spots and not look back.** The "overlook and ignore" strategy is good for occasional lapses. Don't sweat the small stuff. But every couple will find themselves in one or more recurring arguments. **The first year of Marriage is a cliche for a reason.** In the close confines of Marriage, interrelated and interdependent, the other person sees *all those things we have never* (perhaps with good reason) *let other people see about us*. The other person is on the other end, not just of our good days, but of our bad days. When we depend on each other in *every* way…well, things can start to unravel a bit. Feelings fray, tempers flare. We start feeling things about our partner we do not want to feel. Expectations can be trampled. The urge to protect what remains of the good life can be…well, we've all been there. More often than not, couples accumulate recurring issues over time. What are the recurring issues in your Marriage?

_____

_____

_____

_____

…for your Father knows what you need before you ask Him.
MATTHEW 6:8

WE MUST *LEARN HOW TO UNDERSTAND* EACH OTHER:

When we first try to love, we do the things for others *we would like*—a weed-eater for her birthday, a trip to the opera for him. This may be very different from what the other wants or needs. To love as God loves, we must know another as well as we know ourselves. Getting-to-know-you takes awhile. Do you have a funny story about a *real effort to do something loving* that just did not connect?

_____

_____

Simple misunderstandings may not be that simple. We often impute motives and agendas to words or actions based on prior experience. It is vital to learn "reflective listening" to subtract this unnecessary source of conflict. If a person takes offense at an action or words, *this person must reflect back to the doer what they believe the doer intended to communicate*. If words or actions were misunderstood, the process is repeated until the doer agrees that this is what was intended. Of course, sometimes we send mixed messages. We may need to clean up what was done or said to make our message clear. **Better learning, listening, communicating and doing will take care of quite a few issues…but not all.** What role has misunderstanding played in your Marriage?

_____

_____

_____

_____

In your anger do not sin.
EPHESIANS 4:26

*...if anyone is caught in any transgression, you who are spiritual should restore him
in a spirit of gentleness. Keep watch on yourself, lest you, too, be tempted.*
GALATIANS 6:1 (ENGLISH STANDARD VERSION)[6]

CONFLICTS: THE DOORWAY TO GROWTH AND TRANSFORMATION

Many people view rough spots as unfavorable things and fights as purely destructive. Marriage counselors recommend learning to "fight fair," and teach conflict resolution skills to minimize the damage. What if I suggested to you, in contrast, that these conflicts are actually not a bad thing at all? What if I suggested that these are the doorway to the very *personal growth and transformation* that will create *the best relationship in the long run*? If, that is, **these things are approached according to God's Covenant plan.** There are innumerable conflict scenarios in Marriage. Instead of choosing one, let us look at general principles. You can apply these to specific situations. There is a lengthy section in *The Covenant of Marriage* on this vital topic.

DIAGNOSE THE SOURCE OF CONFLICT

Many sources of conflict are breaches of Covenant. It is helpful to **identify the Covenant ideals and the Scriptural principles** in any conflict situation. Often something *unloving according to God's definition* has prompted a reaction. **At this point the doer may own the problem, repent, and correct.** The problem may be straightforward: *learn* the right thing to do, make it a *priority, commit* to do it, and *get it done.* Employ our three powers—strengthening them in the process—and solve the problem.

Or, the doer may justify the words, attitude, or action. A fight often results. This is the scenario we want to focus on as the doorway to growth for both parties. Often both people start trying to justify their position. Both want to be *right.* **What God wants is for both people to de-construct this situation, then craft the most constructive approach as *partners and allies*.** There is a learning curve to get to this point, but it is possible to develop this pattern. When we do, this will become the doorway to many deep and wonderful things in Marriage. The agenda of both must shift from being right to ***getting it right.*** Both are to seek the greatest benefit for both parties.

You were taught, with regard to your former way of life, to put off your old self,
which is being corrupted by its deceitful desires; to be made new in the attitude of your minds;
and to put on the new self, created to be like God in true righteousness and holiness.
Ephesians 4:22-24

Before looking for a solution, let us take a closer look at the totality of the problem. *Why* does one person engage in a pattern that is out-of-bounds? Or, why does one have expectations which, if unmet, result in conflict? Or, *why* do two people have completely different agendas, values, or goals which both are determined to implement? Or, *why* does someone routinely forget important things, or fail to follow through, or display other dysfunctional patterns that are a source of recurring conflict? Obviously **the person has made peace with this pattern, but the spouse has not, nor should he or she.** Why do you think these patterns exist?

_____

_____

Go and make disciples...teaching them to obey everything I have commanded you.
Matthew 28:19-20

If anyone loves me, he will obey my teachings. My Father will love him,
and we will come to him and make our home with him.
John 14:23

We all have a guidance system created by God for one purpose: to direct us toward the wisest moves that produce the best outcomes. God intends that this system be based on **actual truth**. Thus, we are **led by Him and His truth**. If so, we will build an intimate relationship with Him and be used by Him. What would it be like if every move we made was *led by God and His truth*? What would your Marriage be like if you both consistently followed God's leading?

_____

_____

TWO PARTS OF *US* DETERMINE THE LIFE WE BUILD

Our **guidance system** forms our *sense of self-interest*, as well as our *habits, values, priorities, goals, preferences, desires, ideals, viewpoints, attitudes,* and many of our *feelings*. **Our agenda in every area of life** is formed by all of the above. The foundation of all of these, again, are **beliefs we have embraced.** Our guidance system builds much of our external life.

A related part of us consists of *qualities we develop*—**our character.** Are we kind or crass, generous or greedy, good natured or hateful, honest or manipulative? **Character** can be defined as what other people—based on experience—reasonably expect of us and what we expect from ourselves. Our character forms much of **our approach to life,** and much of our **experience of life.** One person takes calculated risks, is enthusiastic and optimistic; another is fearful, withdrawn, and depressed. These two people build different things in life, and experience life differently. They even experience the *same circumstances* differently. How is character built? *It is also built upon ideas we embraced, but of a different sort.* These are ideas about **who we are** or **should be.** If being honest works for us early on, we build our integrity. If lies and deception seem to work better for us, dishonesty becomes part of our persona. Many people think they have been *formed by their life experiences.* Another factor is often unrecognized: what we **concluded was true** about ourselves and life **based on these experiences.** Two people can draw completely different conclusions from identical circumstances. People then live out these conclusions going forward. What has formed your character and your guidance system?

OUR TRUE IDENTITY

There is a third part of us that *directs our life and determines our destiny*—**our true identity**. In our day *we often confuse our true self with our preferences, or with our character.* But our guidance system and our character are both built on decisions. These are not *fixed in stone* as our true identity is. We can change any element of the former, but change nothing about our true identity. **Our identity includes all of our innate potential, the ways we are hard-wired (visual or auditory learner, intelligence, artistic or athletic potential, and many other things), and our conscious being, the me who longs to be known and loved.** We spend our entire lives trying to figure out who we are—mostly looking in the eyes of those around us. We learn our place in the world through experience. *What potential do we have to develop, and do we have what it takes to succeed?* **We live out who we believe ourselves to be.** Note: we just discussed two very different things—*who we actually are, and who we believe we are based on feedback and experience.* Could we be mis-informed about who we really are? If so, how do you think this would impact our life?

BUILDING OUR MIS-GUIDANCE SYSTEM

Everything we do, say, or think on a given day comes ultimately from our character or our guidance system. Our **guidance system** is based on ideas that *we previously embraced*—which may be true or false. Our **character** is based on what we *think we are supposed to be and what we think works best*—based on limited experience and the ideas from our world. What if these parts of our life **are not based on truth, the best ideas, and an accurate understanding of who we are**? Since these things *direct the course of our lives,* what happens to our lives and our relationships? Do relationships suffer—and do we suffer?

What if we are misguided? We head the wrong way down the path. We will be in some way unfaithful to our Covenant. What if we *built things into our character* that do not work well? Same thing—we will not live in harmony with Covenant. *What if we are living down to our view of ourselves* instead of living up to who God made us to be? This will show up as an *inability to love as God directs.* As we look at ourselves, **we have made peace with the whole package**—with all our compromises and dysfunctions. We say, "This is just me." But is this true? Are these problem areas set in stone, **or is each subject to revision?**

OUR MISGUIDANCE DETECTOR—CONFLICT

God has issued us a wonderful instrument to detect Covenant violations that a person would otherwise overlook in themselves—our Covenant partner. An alarm goes off. **Push-back occurs.** God intends that each person *assume responsibility* in Covenant, and adjust behavior accordingly. The one offended is also subject to the same Covenant standards. **We act in accord with Covenant, and also react in accord.** And we bring our expectations into accord. All of this is a learning curve for everyone. A couple can use a conflict to see *who gets their way* about who does the dishes. Or, each can use this opportunity to reflect and learn. "What do I really want?" "Why is this so important to me?" "Why am I acting or reacting like this?" "What does faithfulness to Covenant look like in this situation?" "What does loving my beloved look like here?" How can we resolve these situations in the most constructive way possible?

How many opinions do people have which **are completely misguided**, or *perhaps outright insane?* Yet, people buy into these ideas because they believe *this idea* is **the best move** in a situation—like drug use, gang membership, or harming themselves for a YouTube post…or having an affair. No one gets up in the morning saying, "Today I am going to completely screw up my life." Yet many do. Simply note: **any behavior**—functional or dysfunctional—exists because the person embraced an idea as true. It could not be more obvious that embracing an idea as true does not ensures that it is.

To build the best life or Marriage *the ideas upon which our guidance system is based* that are *not true must shift to actual truth.* Since we think **all** of our embraced ideas are true, how can we separate real truth from false truth? False truths, when lived out, lead to Covenant violations, dysfunction, damage, and conflict. We need to be aware of this reality in ourselves, and lovingly help our beloved recognize these things. We spoke in the last lesson of **the source for truth**, against which every other idea can be measured—and accepted or rejected. What hope do God's plan and His Word offer us when conflict is eroding our Marriage?

Instead, speaking the truth in love, we will grow to become in every respect
the mature body of Him who is Head, that is, Christ.
EPHESIANS 4:15

You are on *the receiving end* of a behavior that needs revision. You *bring it to the doer's attention.* But, **the search for truth** and **the process of implementing it belong to the doer.** This is not something another person can do *for* us, even within Covenant. Any effort to force this process to occur will be counterproductive. The three powers are reserved to each person and *can only be wielded by him or her.* Dysfunctional patterns are a *misuse of our three powers* which **we alone** can correct. A problem area can be identified and change requested, but this is not a police or judicial action. We approach these problems as partners, not adversaries. Patience is a virtue. Usually there is something to be learned by both people. Even if an issue is purely one-sided, be assured that the shoe will be on the other foot soon enough. Treat the other in ways you want to enjoy when it is your turn! Covenant cuts both ways.

And do not be conformed to this world, but be transformed by the renewing of your mind
so that you may prove what the will of God is, that which is good and acceptable and perfect.
ROMANS 12:2 (NASB)

Only let us live up to what we have already attained.
PHILIPPIANS 3:16

You have likely noted some **recurring themes** in this series of lessons. The difference between: 1.) **what we perceive and what is real**; 2.) **what we believe** and **what is true**; 3.) the guidance system **we have** as we enter Marriage and the guidance system **we need** to build the best Marriage; and 4.) the person **we were prior to entering Covenant** and the person **we have the opportunity to become.** We are transformed as we enter Covenant. But we must engage in a process of growth and transformation in order to bring our *expressed life* into line with our *actual identity* and our *relationship.* The fully mature person is faithful to spouse and Covenant in every way. This person is fully obedient to God—especially His two greatest commands: *to love Him* with whole heart, single mind, entire soul, and fullness of strength. Second, *to love others*—especially one's spouse—in the same way. **The good news for those of us who are not there yet? God has a plan to build the best Marriage, the best life, and the best us—called Covenant.**

THE SOURCE OF MISGUIDANCE

These themes raise a question. If there are so many ideas we can embrace that are *not true*, **where did these ideas come from and why would we embrace them?** This may seem like an odd discussion if we simply want a better Marriage. But I assure you, **this topic is vital to understand if we are to build the best Marriage!** Why? The issues we are highlighting involve *actual truth* versus *things that are not true.* What is the opposite of truth? A lie. **We have an enemy standing in the way of our building process,** called the *father of lies* (John 8:44). We must understand this enemy—his *impact,* his strategy, and *the way to overcome his influence.* If we do not understand these things his **strategy of destruction will go unchecked.** Let's drop by the home of a married couple—the first married couple, in fact. What can Adam and Eve can teach us about this enemy's influence in their lives—and ours? Where did it all begin?

THE GARDEN OF EDEN: ADAM AND EVE, TRUTH AND DECEPTION

As we analyze the following conversation, remember that the situation involved Adam and Eve. Though this is Eve's conversation, the mind and heart issues we will highlight are not a male-female thing. They are a human thing. Following the creation of Eve in a one-flesh state with Adam, she had a conversation with a being who did not bother to introduce himself. He offered Eve what sounded like "insider information" about her Creator, the God she had loved and worshipped until this point without question. What did Satan offer Eve in the conversation recorded in Genesis 3:1-13? He pretended to offer *the truth about God.* Her Creator withheld the best option from her because He is that kind of Being (v. 1). Eve leaps to God's defense in verse 2—sort of—but we can see this innuendo about God's character bothered her. In her defense of God she actually misquotes Him. In fact, her words created a scenario in which she could appear to discredit God as well—by touching "the tree of the knowledge of good and evil" and not dying on the spot. God said not to eat the fruit, but nothing about touching the tree. Adam and Eve could build a tree house in the tree if they liked. But, if they *ate the fruit* they would die.

Aware that Eve's confidence in God was shaken (Genesis 3:3), Satan unveils his real plan for her—*to disobey God.* He *offered something wonderful* if she would do as he suggested. His innuendo changed to accusation: God is a liar. "You will surely not die. For God knows that when you eat of it your eyes will be opened, and you will be like God, knowing good and evil." Note carefully the offered benefit—to become "like God." Would Eve desire this promotion? Does this desire explain the rest of the story? Let us see. Is this a promotion humans have aspired to ever since? Where in our world do you see people desiring to be "as God?"

_____

_____

Eve's next step is truly fascinating, not only in light of her story, but in light of all of our stories. She engaged in the first scientific experiment ever recorded, at least science as it would be defined today. First, she discounted the reality of God's revelation (what He said would happen if she ate the fruit). What remains? She was left with her own powers of observation. So, Eve examined the fruit. "When the woman saw that the fruit of the tree was good for food and pleasing to the eye, and also desirable for gaining wisdom…" (v. 6). If we do not take spiritual realities into account, what do we base our decisions on?

_____

_____

Now we arrive at **the focal point of the situation,** the same point we discuss throughout the *Covenant* series, the same place we will all be innumerable times throughout our lives: **we come to the point of decision.** Until this point it was just words. All of us go back and forth in our minds about situations. We consider, we ponder, we assess the relative merits of things we hear. We try to understand our desires and needs. We assign various weighs to all these factors, then try to make the best choice. In this entire process there is one defining moment: the moment when a decision is rendered and action results. **At this point the consequences of the decision are unleashed, for better or worse.** These consequences may follow us, may shape and define us, or perhaps haunt us for the rest of our lives. Has anyone ever had buyer's remorse? Have we ever wanted something so badly that we ignored objections we knew somewhere down inside were really true? We ran over this guardrail on the way off a cliff as we chased something so important, so desirable—at least we thought it was. When the reality of the situation becomes apparent and we are headed toward a painful landing, what do we say? "If I had only *listened to…*" Have you ever had such a moment? How did you realize you had been deceived?

We can envision Eve leaning against the tree as she studied the fruit. Then, she reached up and touched it. Perhaps she snapped off the stem and held the fruit in her hand, looking closely. She smelled, felt, perhaps squeezed a little. At a superficial level her decision was about one thing: *whom did she really believe?* She was already far down the path toward disbelief in God's words. At a deeper level, though, her decision came down to **choosing one of two ways of thinking:** whom did she have **the most reason to believe;** or whom did she most **want to believe?** Did Eve have more reason to believe her Creator? Or, should she trust this unfamiliar creature who suggested that her Creator's intentions were not what she thought? Was God really not worthy of trust? Or, was she being truly observant and analytical? Did she consider her entire life? From the time her eyes first opened beside her husband, lover, and best friend in a world perfectly suited to her, could she find **any reason** to not trust God? The only time she ever questioned His love was right here, right now, based solely upon the words of a this unknown being.

A vital element is in play here, beyond what is factual and what is not: **desire.** Eve was open to Satan's ideas because *she thought her eyes were being opened to new possibilities,* very desirable possibilities. As a result, Eve narrowed her examination of reality down to a single question. The answer she chose reinforced her move away from trusting in God. *The fruit simply did not appear to be as dangerous as God said it was.* In fact, it looked….good to her, thus good for her. This lined up with the words of her new best friend and confidant. Perhaps he was right when he told her God was holding back the best things from her. After considering all of the above, Eve exercised her most fundamental human prerogative (and all of her three powers). She made her decision, then raised the fruit to her lips (v. 6). Have you ever been thoroughly convinced you were right, but were not? What role did *your desire* play in this situation?

Rather than entering the wonderful new life she was promised, Eve soon discovered that every idea offered by her new BFF was a lie. Truth and reality are synonymous at the deepest level. Truth is simply a statement of reality, an accurate description of the cause-and-effect universe God created for us to inhabit. Eve would find that everything God said about eating the fruit was true. God's truth, His Word, has been spoken to humanity throughout history. But since the very beginning there has been another voice. This voice spews out innumerable reasons why we should not *believe*, **not believe in**, our Creator or His Word. **We get to choose between these two voices.** Unfortunately, we often embrace the words of **the one who appears to us to offer the best future, rather than the One who truly does.**

THE POWER OF DECEPTION

To defend our lives and Marriages and build them to their potential, we must understand **the power of deception**. Deception is not just a lie. It is *an offer* of something we become persuaded is an important upgrade, something necessary for our best life. In order to receive the promised benefit, though, this offer *always requires us to depart from God's path*. This, by the way, *is the point of this entire exercise*. To pull us away from God, Satan's representatives offer us something God does not offer in His plan. Something *we decide* justifies our brushing past God as we reach out for something…so wonderful…until we find that it is not. Promised benefits never materialize, or are not what we expected.

In the Genesis story we are dissecting the thoughts and heart processes of Eve because God recounts her conversation with Satan. What was going on in Adam's mind and heart? We are not told. It is evident, though, that he did not trust in God and follow Him, or protect his wife. Adam turned and followed the words of Satan, joining in his rebellion. Whatever we are thinking and feeling, we **sell ourselves** in these transactions and **wound our relationship with God.** In our minds this is not about turning away from God per se; we want the glorious future promised to us. But this future is promised to us by a being proven to be a liar throughout human history. Have you ever been deceived like this? Were you aware of the damage this would do to your relationship with God on the front end? Or, did you only realize this when you knew you had been deceived?

Do not be conformed to this world…
ROMANS 12:2

Anyone who chooses to be a friend of the world becomes an enemy of God.
JAMES 4:4

Why does Scripture speak of "the world" as a singular thing, and a source of uniformly bad guidance? As something, in its entirety, that is *diametrically opposed to the leadership of God*? We look at diversity as an exercise in human creativity, as different approaches to solve the same problems, or perhaps cultures having different problems to solve. Perhaps we should reconsider revering and embracing such diversity. Let us examine the source of the misguidance which has characterized human civilization from the beginning. Our culture's ideas are not new—there is literally nothing new under the sun. Once we see *the source of these ideas*, and *the motive behind them,* we may begin to view ideas *other than God's* differently. We may begin to view them as Eve should have viewed Satan's offer. What do you think is meant by the term "the world?"

Adam and Eve lived long ago in a very different world. What can we learn from this encounter that is of value for our lives? Is our world—so different in some ways—still being influenced by spiritual beings with the same agenda? How could this be, since we are so scientific, advanced, and educated? We are taught to view anything of the spiritual realm—now or in the past—as a *myth*. A myth by definition is not real. What evidence suggests that this same influence is at work in our world? In our own lives?

People in Christian circles speak of being tempted by Satan or influenced by him. He must really get around, since he is a created being, a fallen angel who can only be in one place at one time. Here, we will look briefly at the process by which Satan and his followers have influenced humanity throughout history. This point is laid out in much more detail in *What Is a Covenant?* by this author. The point of this information is to explain how—and how extensively—the enemies of God have influenced humanity from the time of Adam and Eve until today's evening news. One of Satan's most powerful weapons is the belief that he does not exist.

The Nephilim were on the earth in those days—and also afterward—
when the sons of God went to the daughters of men and had children by them.
GENESIS 6:4

Genesis 6:1-7 describes an event in brief that is recounted in much greater detail in the Book of Enoch, an ancient Jewish history book quoted several times by New Testament writers. According to both sources the "sons of God" (perhaps better translated "sons of heaven"—fallen angels, or Watchers), came to earth, mated with human women, and produced offspring. A parallel historical account is provided by extensive writings from the first human civilization—in Sumeria, which began roughly 6,000 years ago. Sumerian writings speak of *gods* who ruled over them, procreated with them, and taught them everything they knew of the "arts of civilization." In addition to their writings, temples decorated with images of these "gods," often depicted with wings, attest to their worship of this pantheon—or group—of gods.

The Lord saw how great man's wickedness on the earth had become,
and that every inclination and the thoughts of his heart were only evil all the time.
GENESIS 6:5

For all the gods of the nations are idols; but the Lord made the heavens.
I CHRONICLES 16:26

Or simply, Genesis 6 and the Book of Enoch describe fallen angels corrupting the entire earth. Angels are not mortal. They do not die. The pantheon of gods first worshipped by the Sumerians has also been very durable. These "gods" are seen in every ancient civilization, and even in some current cultures. In ancient cultures the leaders ruled in the name of these gods. Virtually all ancient cultures with written records describe similar beings who conveyed knowledge to humans, required worship from them, and often ruled over them. These beings go by different name in different civilizations, but there were always a similar number of principle gods who played similar roles. Inanna—goddess of fertility, marriage, and prostitution of the Sumerians—became Ishtar of the Babylonians, then Aphrodite of the Greeks, then Venus of the Romans. Why did fallen angels *fall*? What does Satan want? To be worshipped. Would it be surprising if his followers passed themselves off as gods? If so, would these beings likely convey a way of life to humans that opposed the rule and rules of God?

But how could these ancient events impact us? We refer to our civilization as "Western Civilization." Why? Because in many ways we follow a way of life handed down to us from the Greeks, by way of the Romans. This way of life includes such things as our concept of democracy. Where did the Greeks and Romans get their way of life? According to early Greek writings, from the Babylonians, whose early writings in turn attribute their way of life to the Sumerians. All of these cultures worshipped—and took seriously—the edicts of their gods. Our culture is also heavily salted with ideas from our Judeo-Christian heritage—truths from God. But much of our cultural mentality—a growing amount in our day—comes from the values, priorities, and way of life handed down to humanity by these gods. Who are...? The name "Sumeria" in the Sumerian language means "Land of the Watchers." The Scriptures speak of Satan having a degree of real dominion over the earth. How well does this spiritual reality correlate with human history or current events? What influence might Satan and his forces wield in our culture? We do not have temples and conduct sacrifices to these beings...do we? Here is a hint: look for things going on in our culture that depart from God's ways, or oppose Him outright, and carefully consider the origin of these ideas. It is also worth noting that Adam and Even did not build a temple or conduct a sacrifice. They simply bought into Satan's ideas and followed his leadership.

> *They sacrificed their sons and daughters to false gods...to the demons.*
> PSALM 106:37

> *You must not worship the gods of these nations or serve t*
> *hem in any way or imitate their evil practices...*
> EXODUS 23:24

> *...for they perform for their gods every detestable act that the Lord hates.*
> DEUTERONOMY 12:31

> *...the sacrifices of pagans are offered to demons...*
> I CORINTHIANS 10:20

Why is *this* in a book on Marriage? We are talking about good and true ideas *from God*, versus *other* ideas—false ideas, deceptive ideas—*from where*? The Scriptures say, "the world." **But what exactly is the world, and which ideas come from there?** Worship of these beings continues in many places. Thor now has movies. But worship of these beings is not just about building temples and conducting sacrifices. It is about embracing ideas offered by these beings, about following the leadership of these creatures—away from God. We do not have a temple to Inanna down the street, but our culture is certainly embracing her view of sexuality.[7]

Let us think for a moment about the character and agenda of the enemy—so we will recognize his fingerprints. He wants to **upend every part of God's order**. He wants to assume ultimate power, and wants everyone to be accountable to him. He wants to upend the moral universe—good is wrong, evil is right. He wants to sit as judge of the universe and ordain a system of law that is the opposite of God's. Satan has no positive or creative plan; his only agenda is *not-God*. Those who follow him are devoted to these things, and devoted to influencing others to join in this rebellion. Even those who want to follow God may be deceived into going along with this rebellious agenda—by embracing its ideas. In Marriage, God calls us to love. What would Satan like to see in your Marriage? Are Satan's fingerprints on anything in your Marriage?

_____

_____

Does all of ***not God*** represent deception sown into our world by beings intent on inflicting as much damage as possible on those made in God's image? Is our world moving ever closer to the brink of destruction from any of a dozen causes because of only human idiocy, or is a more sinister agenda behind all this destruction? An agenda that arises in the spiritual realm—from Satan and one third of all angels who follow his leadership? If this is the case, as I believe it is, **we have every reason to carefully review everything we think we know about living** courtesy of our culture or any culture. We have every reason to compare these ideas with objective truth revealed to us by God, and **every possible motivation to reject and eject ideas that have been sold to us purely for the purpose of damaging us.** How would you go about making this comparison?

_____

_____

_____

The heart of God's Covenant plan is to ***shift the foundation for our guidance system from the lies of the world to His truth.*** God wants our Marriages to bear testimony to a watching world of the abundant lives and blessed Marriages that are built by following Him. This, in contrast to the challenged and dysfunctional lives and Marriages produced by following the lies of His enemies. Any life and any Marriage draws from both sources. We are often unaware of the author of a particular idea unless we dust for fingerprints. If we want to improve our Marriage, does this point to an obvious strategy? For any idea we base our lives upon, the first question should be, **"Who authored this idea?"** This question can always be answered by reviewing the Scriptures.

If you know someone is trying to manipulate you, con you, use or abuse you, how do you listen to a *wonderful offer* from this person?

_____

_____

If you *truly believe* in someone, if you are completely confident he or she *has your best interest in mind,* how do you listen to a wonderful offer from this person?

_____

_____

_____

Who really has your best interest in mind—God or His enemies? Is there ever any confusion on this point?

_____

_____

_____

What is *the world,* and what advice is it offering you about your life and Marriage?

_____

_____

_____

_____

_____

How do you think advice from the world will turn out in the end? Why?

_____

_____

_____

LESSON EIGHT

RENEWING OUR MINDS WITH TRUTH
and BUILDING CONVICTIONS

Early in Marriage I noticed something important. I was passionately in love with my wife and wanted to show it in every way possible. However, on several occasions there were good things I might have done that *I did not do.* Why? Because, in my estimation, what I was called on to do *violated my sense of self-interest* to an unacceptable point. Faced with the decision between *loving another* and *self-interest,* self-interest won. As I thought more about this inner conflict I realized that my sense of self-interest might be worth a second look. What other priority was so important? What was I trying to hold on to—instead of loving my wife in action? I was following directives that came from ideas embraced decades earlier. "*This* is how to get and keep the best for yourself." But, as I looked at what I was doing—and not doing—this now made no sense. This was my introduction to **my guidance system,** and one of the many ways it can malfunction and do damage. Something needed to change, but what? And how? Have you ever had to **decide between self-interest and love**? Which side won?

_____

_____

*Do your best to present yourself to God as one approved, a worker who does
not need to be ashamed, who correctly handles the word of truth.*
II Timothy 2:15

*Opponents must be gently instructed, in the hope that God will grant them repentance
leading to a knowledge of the truth, and that they will come to their senses and
escape from the trap of the devil, who has taken them captive to do his will.*
II Timothy 2:25-26

Sanctify them by the truth; your word is truth.
John 17:17

Then another insight clicked into place that came from years of personal spiritual growth and mentoring. When God tells us to "be transformed" (Romans 12:2) this does not mean we are to *wait on God to transform us* so we *want to do different things.* Instead, **God is inviting us to embrace His truth and live it out in specific ways.** I was familiar with this process, since I had applied Scriptural truths in other areas of life. This same process could be employed for truths related to Marriage—specific Scriptures and the overall truths of God's Covenant plan. When you want to apply a truth from God to your life, how do you do so?

_____

_____

_____

You will know the truth and the truth will set you free.
JOHN 8:32

The word "know" in this context is a covenant term. "To know" means to understand an idea. But another meaning is to *have sexual relations with,* which involves **someone becoming part of us** at the deepest level. When used in Scripture, this word means more than head-knowledge. It means to **embrace the idea, so it becomes part of us.** We use our *power of affirmation* to **receive it as our truth.** Going forward, this idea directs our behavior and adjusts our guidance system. If we embrace truth, what are we set *free from*? From **damage to self and others** caused by misguided behavior, and **the consequences of such behavior** that accumulate in our lives. We are freed from **the internal conflict** of knowing one thing is right, but being driven by some unseen internal force toward another decision. **We are now free to walk with God** on His path for our lives—the path to the best relationship with Him, the best life, and the best relationships. We see this impact powerfully in our Marriage. Are there things in your Marriage, or in your heart, *from which you would like to be set free?*

_____

_____

Imagine a person with several ropes tied around his or her torso. These ropes lead in different directions, and pull the person one way, then another. If the person tries to move in a direction, what happens? Have you ever felt like this in your life? You want to move toward, say, a better relationship. But unseen forces are pulling you in other directions. What happens next? Often, nothing much—we feel stuck. We often believe we are a victim of *outside forces.* **We are often unaware of the internal forces opposing our progress.** Have you ever felt like this? What ropes are pulling you away from what you want?

_____

_____

Have you ever seen a person **stuck in a dysfunctional pattern**, whose choices clearly play a role in this pattern? People are often not aware of their own role. *Often, they view themselves as a victim, period*. But from a distance you see a different picture. This pattern is created by living out something he or she embraced as true. If a person believes that he or she is a loser, or deserves bad outcomes, guess what happens next? Despite the fact that the person is capable of building a better life, *you will see a pattern of self-sabotage*. The person subliminally engineers one negative life outcome after another. People build a life that corresponds to *who and what they think they are*. **Does God want to free us from this bondage?** What is His plan to do this? **First, to transform us at the deepest level. Then, to teach us to live out the truth of our transformation, and of truth itself.** All we must do is review and revise our guidance system and character. Piece of cake…if you know how, and are sufficiently motivated. Actually, there is a learning curve for this, as for any important thing in life. The first step is to identify the dysfunctional pattern, then the idea that led to the pattern. *Once we identify the offending idea, let's see how we can shift to a different guiding idea.*

A FIVE STEP PROCESS FOR LIFE CHANGE

There are many approaches proven over the last 2,000 years to **bring our lives into better alignment with God's Word, will, and heart.** Here is one approach that has proven extremely helpful in most situations—in the lives of people I have mentored and taught for forty-plus years, and in my own life.

The plan is to use the truth—God's revelations in Scripture—to reprogram our guidance system. Any "truth" arising from any human or group benefits from a *Berean review*. This includes any system of theology or the view of any denomination. Every belief should *firmly rest upon the whole counsel of God—all the Scriptures on a given topic*. If it does not, our beliefs should shift to include everything God believes is true.

We benefit from knowing the guardrails and keeping our freedom in Christ in view. This means finding the out-of-bounds lines, beyond which we violate God's Word. Then, viewing everything between these guardrails as a matter of conscience between the individual and God. We can seek direction from God about where along this spectrum He wants us to be. In light of these overall truths, **we seek the truth God wants us to apply** in a given situation. With the Bible topical search tools now available, this is much easier than when I began doing this forty years ago (before the internet was born). I used a Topical Bible, a Chain Reference Bible, and a concordance to locate applicable Scriptures. It takes time and effort to search out truth in God's Word. The question is, "Are we motivated enough to do this?" I realized early on that the life I sought in Christ is found only by building more and more of my life upon God's truth. This motivated me to make the search for truth one of the highest priorities in my life. What about you?

_____

_____

The following pattern is *even more helpful if written down* for careful consideration and later review. Over the next week, try this pattern out with an issue you face in your Marriage—something you would like to see out of your life, or something you would like to see in your life. We want to move from Point A, where we are now, to Point B, consistently living out God's truth in our Marriage. What issue or life change will you choose?

_____

_____

1.) **Identify the truth.** Write down all pertinent Scriptures and *carefully study the exact wording* of each. Look up words in English or the original language to make sure you have the full truth of the matter. Now you know *precisely what God says* about a topic. Then, **ask God what He is saying to you** about this situation. Write down this truth. This is not just *the* truth; this is *your truth from God for this situation.* Consider for a moment what is happening here. The God of the universe and Creator of all is speaking to you about a detail of your life. How important a thing is this? What priority should you give this information? It is vital to not merely hear this truth, but *embrace it*! What truth did God show you? Will you embrace it?

_____

_____

2.) **What is my life like now?** Fascinating things almost always go on inside me when I confront this question. As I see the truth and ask myself, "How am I doing with this one?", almost always my first answer is, *"Pretty well, in fact."* If this were true, why would God bother…? Instead of accepting this answer, if I settle in and *quietly let God show me what He wants me to know,* suddenly I begin to see other layers, dimensions and applications of this truth. Often I am near tears when I see how far I am from God's desire, and how much damage my blindness has caused in my life or the lives of others. I now see Point A—where I am now—clearly. Where are you in relation to the truth God showed you?

_____

_____

3.) **What should my life be like?** This same insight extends to what we *should be doing, thinking, feeling, etc.,* according to God's Word. This is point B. Describe this in as much detail as possible. What does God want to see in you and your life?

_____

_____

4.) **What must happen to move from Point A to Point B?** A series of steps will be needed in order to consistently choose B instead of A. Lay out a step-by-step plan, so you will know *exactly what you need to do.* With habit patterns we are often in the middle of the situation—and have repeated the undesired pattern—before we realize what is happening. The first step is to *see the situation coming.*

Next, we may need to repeat a truth, quote a Scripture, review our step-by-step plan, or stop and pray. We may need to consider the outcome we do not want. As we follow these steps on several occasions and see better outcomes, our guidance system will choose our new path with less effort. The new pattern will soon feel like *us*. A new habit is born. What steps do you need to build your new habit?

_____

_____

5.) **Checkup and accountability.** This may be the **most vital step** to successfully build a new life pattern. Why? We may be excited about a new idea, but attention will soon *shift to the next new thing*. In my Christian life countless things have impacted me and moved me, things I was convinced God was speaking to me about…but later, when I encountered this same point, I had only a vague recollection of it. The idea had gone in one ear, then quickly out the other. As James said, I became *a forgetful hearer* (James 1:25). Instead, schedule a review far enough out so there will be a few events to examine to check our progress. We can amend our plan to improve results. If we involve a trusted person *to hold us* accountable we are often more motivated (one tip—do not involve your spouse in this capacity if the issue is between the two of you—use a same-sex friend). When will you schedule a checkup for your progress on the issue you chose?

_____

_____

To produce a new life pattern we need *repetition plus reinforcement*. The key is to stay with the revision process until you are consistently successful. Then, schedule another review in, say, six months. A journal is helpful, so we can look back at previous issues and review them. Seeing our progress over months and years is very encouraging. We put issues behind us, but never run out of new ones. Early in my Christian life I (Mark) found myself fighting the same battles over and over—to the point of discouragement, then desperation. The solution to my desperation was learning to grow spiritually, to revise my guidance system with God's truth. As I experienced the benefits of this, it built a life-long drive in me to find and apply truth in every area of life. If we continue this process, we grow. If our spouse is involved in the same process, and we aid each other on our respective journeys, we grow together. As we grow together, we grow closer. We become better people who can build better relationships. How can you make this plan an even bigger part of your Marriage?

_____

_____

Master, you entrusted me with five talents...See, I have gained five more.
His Master replied, "...you have been faithful with a few things;
I will put you in charge of many things...Come and share your Master's happiness."
MATTHEW 25:20-21

THE CURRICULUM OF LIFE

How do we know what we need to revise? Do not worry. **God designed a program for your growth and transformation: a spouse and a Marriage.** There will be no shortage of issues that come one after another, or occasionally in groups. Not all involve conflict. Some are life circumstances you will sort out together. Some involve personal patterns that can be improved. Some life situations require us to develop new strategies and coping skills. Holley and I have spent countless hours discussing life on this level, trouble-shooting not only situations, but ourselves. The result? The wisdom, character, and perspective gained as we *grow together* has created **an experience of life and a Marriage so desirable** that we want to write books about it. These blessing are all from God, to be sure. But these blessings come largely in the form of *opportunities* which involve devotion and sweat on our part. God's choicest blessings flow from **faithfulness** to God, to His truth, and to the opportunity to build the life He created within us, and the one-flesh relationship He knit together. *Faithfulness on our part* is God's love language. Faithfulness is the key that unlocks the door to His blessings. What blessings have arisen from trials and issues in your Marriage?

_____

_____

_____

_____

BUILDING CONVICTIONS

What are convictions? First, we have **embraced the truth** of a matter. But we also recognize that **this is the only acceptable position for us.** We may embrace God's truth about something, but what happens to our previously-affirmed ideas? Do these evaporate in the presence of God's truth? Unfortunately, no. We now have **two conflicting ideas to choose from** for guidance. We have become what the Scriptures call "double-minded" (James 1:8). Does this explain *seemingly inexplicable behavior* occasionally seen in mature Christians—who know full well that *something is wrong*, but do it anyway? Another embraced idea—a deceptive idea—says, "Yes, but in this situation this is still your best move." An embraced idea remains on our "acceptable in some circumstances" list—*unless we remove it.* In order to have a conviction about something, we *not only embrace the truth*, but must also sift through our guidance system. We must **brand any conflicting ideas as the lie that they are.** What we previously affirmed we can *dis-affirm.* Now we will make *only a single choice on a matter*, with no acceptable alternative. We will not compromise or change our position regardless of a threat made or the price paid. Many have been martyred for refusing to deny Jesus as Lord. Others were imprisoned for refusing to compromise the truth of God. God says He will reward such devotion. He uses these displays of commitment powerfully in the lives of others. We admire people who take strong, perhaps costly stands on issues that are important to God—like Marriage. What role do convictions play in your Marriage?

_____

_____

We looked at Adam and Eve's scenario because this same scenario will be part of our lives on a daily basis. **Convictions are decision about life that we pre-make.** We must be continually on guard. We may feel strongly that we will never do something, but deep within there may be images and desires absorbed from our culture that whisper, "Unless…" No one gets up in the morning and says, "Today I am going to do something that will blow my life and family apart." _But many every day get up, go forth and do just that._ A belief lodges in someone's guidance system that such behavior offers something important for his or her life. Where would such an idea come from? It is very helpful to figure out _why we might not want to do such things._ What possible scenarios might we encounter where "no one will know," or we are having a rough patch with our spouse, or we run into that old flame while out of town, or that admiring co-worker in an unguarded moment. In other words, **in order to develop a true conviction we must not only build a strong foundation of what we purpose to do, but an equally strong foundation of what we will not do if given the opportunity.** Why would the behavior in question be the last thing we would ever do, given the opportunity, _regardless of how we feel in the moment?_ **This moves our guidance system away from feelings to our commitments.** And it pre-dismisses Satan's arguments in favor of his deception. In other words, we see this con coming and want to defend our life as if our life depends on it—which it does.

What convictions about Marriage do you want to see in yourself and your spouse?

_____

_____

_____

_____

Now that you have purified yourselves by obeying the truth,
so that you have a sincere love…love one another deeply, from the heart.
I Peter 1:22

COVENANT CONVICTIONS

Once we learn this pattern, we can extend it to every important issue—like never doing or saying anything to dishonor our husband or wife in public or private. To not disrespect them regardless of the situation. One can go down the list we provided from wedding vows and pre-decide how we _will_ and _will not_ treat each other in regard to each topic. Then, when feelings flare, agendas clash, or something important is on the line—if we have developed convictions about how we will treat each other *in any situation*—we can handle serious and delicate situations constructively…instead of creating a bigger problem. This is what God desires. If we do this we will find it is also what we most deeply desire. Why? Because now a potential or real crisis will build our relationship instead of damaging it. We remain allies, and become better friends. Bonds can be strengthened when tested. What Covenant convictions would you like to develop?

_____

_____

_____

_____

BECOMING WHOLEHEARTED

In Scripture we see the terms **double-minded** and **wholehearted**. In James 1 a double-minded person is described as one who believes, but *also doubts*. That is, *this person has affirmed two ideas which are mutually exclusive.* Only one can be true. This person is termed "unstable in all his ways." This is the opposite of a person with convictions, **who has gone through and weeded out such conflicting and contradictory ideas.** James says this person cannot expect to receive anything from God. In Marriage or in life a person with a guidance system full of conflicting ideas cannot consistently follow God's path. They cannot enjoy the blessings of this path or the life it produces. Are you double-minded or wholehearted about your Marriage? Why?

_____

_____

_____

Consider a person with convictions. As we noted, our emotions form around our affirmed truths. If our affirmed truths are based on *actual truth* they will be consistent with each other. They will be *consistent with our inner being*, with *the heart and mind of God*, and with *our moral cause-and-effect universe.* If all this is true, what will be going on in our heart? Our feelings will be coherent. They will be consistent with *who we are, with God, and with realty.* What if our emotions all point in the same direction? This is like the person described earlier with *many ropes tied to their torso.* But this time *the ropes all pull in the same direction,* **the direction of greatest benefit in life.** The direction God desires that we go, the direction of growth, transformation, gratification and satisfaction. This person has a passion for life. This is a powerful person whose life is in balance. This person has a passionate love for God, for husband or wife, for family. Is this your life, or could you envision this becoming your life?

_____

_____

To build this life we must make a habit of developing convictions. Become single-minded on one issue. Then repeat this process for issue after issue, until more and more of life is firmly founded on God's Word, and we are less and less susceptible to Satan's offerings. Consider the quality of this life: inner calm, peace with God, and peace within when dealing with people regardless of the circumstances. This person's peace is not tied to being perfectly loved by people, or to circumstances. Instead, this person's equilibrium comes from being in harmony with God and His purposes. This person's inner life and outer expression of life are in harmony. A person who walks this path and builds this life will be used by God in the lives of many. He or she will reap the rewards of service to God, and enjoy the love and respect of many. What kind of Marriage relationship would this person build?

_____

_____

_____

Is this the kind of Covenant partner you want? What would it take for you to be this kind of Covenant partner to another?

_____

_____

_____

ASSEMBLING THE BUILDING BLOCKS
and USING THE TOOLS GOD GAVE US

The world's advice about Marriage boils down to: "Be nicer; say 'yes' to everything and apologize for… everything." Is this the picture of perfect love? Does God love us perfectly? Does He always say yes to every prayer, ASAP? In fact, doesn't God sometimes say, "No," or "Let's do this instead." Wait, isn't the good life about *getting what we want*? If we do not get what we want, aren't we just settling…? How can someone call this loving? What do you think?

_____

_____

It does not take much life experience to realize that what we want is not always best for us in the long term. Yet, we want what we want because we are *convinced* that a thing is best for us. God gives us several things we can use to cross-check our thoughts and desires: His Word, reality, consequences, life experience, and our wife or husband. What is going on when the two want different things? Different opinions and agendas in a Marriage are not bad things. This just means our opinions merit review. One or both may benefit from revision. This is an opportunity for each to consider *why* something is desired, and match these desires against God's truth. Is this being done in a constructive way in your Marriage?

_____

_____

Now, to Him who is able to do exceedingly abundantly, beyond all we ask or think…
EPHESIANS 3:20

Holley and I do not always say "yes" to each other's requests or agendas, though at this point in our Marriage we often do. Or, we may see things differently. This does not mean someone is wrong. Perhaps we see different things due to different vantage points. We need to talk through and think through issues. We need to search them out in God's Word and pray through them. We are, after all, allies. We are committed to learning, to growing, and to growing together. We do not always end up seeing things the same way, but we have ensured that our views—our priorities, values, goals, and agendas—are on a solid foundation of truth. Therefore, our desires are based on truth. We have not figured out everything in life, or within us—far from it. But we have come a long way. This morning we were talking about all the amazing things God has built in our lives and our Marriage over the decades, things we would not have believed if someone had told us as we began our journey together. "Yes" is not always the best answer. The best answer is always to cross-check the foundation of our thinking. Is it truth? Do you use this approach?_____

How do you compare your ideas with actual truth?

_____

_____

COVENANT AS A PLAN...

We said Covenant is a plan. A plan is a *series of steps* we take. If we are building a house we have a blueprint. This is a picture of the finished product, with a series of smaller pictures that show finer details. An experienced builder can look at a blueprint and also know the *correct order* in which the different pieces are to be built. One cannot tile the bathroom before completing the foundation. We look at the endpoint of the building process—a great Marriage—and want ours to look like this. We want the same color walls and the same woodwork—the parts we can see. We admire the attitude of the two, the ways they treat each other and how they handle problems. But many things were built that we cannot see, things which allow what we do see to exist. God's plan is a lifelong building process covering the whole of life. But certain elements of the foundation must be in place—and built well—for the rest of the structure to be built properly. What is the foundation for a Marriage, and how do we build on this foundation?

Husbands, love your wives as Christ loved the church...and the wife must respect her husband.
Ephesians 5:25-33

*...speaking the truth in love, we will grow to become in every respect
the mature body of Him who is the head, that is, Christ.*
Ephesians 4:15

THREE FOUNDATIONAL ELEMENTS:
COMMITMENT, TRUST, AND RESPECT

You know when someone is in love. He or she cannot stop talking about how wonderful the other is. Precious things of ourselves are entrusted to the other. It is said, "Love is blind," because on occasion such trust is not deserved. But trust is the heart of love. If both prove worthy of trust, respect grows and commitment deepens.

Everything else in a Marriage is built upon the above three elements. Our commitment is founded upon *believing in* one another. This leads to committing ourselves to each other in Covenant—and to the joining and transformation of identity which occurs. God intends our commitment to extend to every area of life. Such *faithfulness* produces respect. But the level of commitment *we display* always remains a choice. Confusing messages about our level of commitment quickly cool a relationship. Clear messages about our commitment warm hearts. Trust is earned by displays of honesty and integrity. A proper working relationship in Marriage requires a high level of trust. The emotional milieu—the inner experience and the emotional interplay—is determined by the level of trust that has been built. True intimacy cannot exist unless complete trust and full confidence have been earned through experience.

Honoring each other is one of our highest duties in Covenant. But we also must prove worthy of being so honored. We do this by being faithful to our partner and to our Covenant, and by conducting ourselves in an honorable manner in all of life. We are never to dishonor the other, but a person can certainly dishonor himself or herself and seriously damage the core of the relationship. The love that we feel for each other over time is directly related to these foundational things. If we want our love to grow, we must pay careful attention to growing our level of commitment, trust, and respect. What does this foundation look like in your Marriage?

_____

_____

THE SEQUENCE OF BUILDING

Certain aspects of behavior and character are vital if we are to build the best Marriage. A split in the wood of a doorframe is annoying and unsightly; a large crack in a foundation can take down the entire house. For large, important buildings, more attention is directed toward the design and construction of the foundation than any other part of the building process. What about a foundation of trust—how is this built, and what is built upon it?

In truthful speech and in the power of God; with weapons of righteousness in the right hand and the left.
II Corinthians 6:7

The standard of truth I am going to commend is far from current cultural practices. We have a choice: do we follow the advice of the world, or the ways of God. Think for a moment how you want to be treated. Do you want to hear the truth? Do you want to be able to trust your spouse? Our culture trains us to treat others in ways we certainly do not want to be treated. Which is why God's instructions begin with, "Do unto others…"

What are your thoughts?

_____

_____

Truthful lips endure forever, but a lying tongue lasts only a moment.
PROVERBS 12:19

Our first obligation is to **align our words with reality,** and to **follow through on our words**. Every word we speak to our husband or wife should be exactly correct, period. When we say we will do something, we should be very careful to do what we say. Granted, circumstances may intervene, but we should avoid saying we will do a thing for the sake of image when we have no intention of doing it. Or, saying we will do something, but being weakly committed to our words and easily diverted. The first step in trust is **teaching the other person that we take our own words seriously.**

When I was first getting to know Holley, I was impressed by her exacting follow-through. If she said she would return a call at a certain time, she called at that time. If she said she would do something, she did it. I quickly learned I could trust her words and rely on her follow-through. How did this matter when I thought of building a serious relationship with her? Have you built this kind of confidence in your spouse? Why or why not?

_____

_____

The next step in relationship is honesty. Our words may be accurate, but accurately describe only part of the story. To build trust we must reveal what we *believe, think, and feel.* We must be interested in the inner life of the one we want to get to know, and reveal our own inner life. Can we safely entrust something to him or her, or does this come back to us as leverage or an attempt to wound? Consider red flags in the realm of trust very carefully! In a healthy growing relationship the two find they can entrust more and more to each other. This is a gradual and mutual process. Each must prove worthy of trust at each level as the relationship deepens. Do trust issues exist in your Marriage? Why or why not?

_____

_____

The next step in relationship is transparency. There is more to our experience of life than facts, what we think, and how we feel. Things like our motivations, goals, dreams, and priorities, and *areas of uncertainty, confusion, fear, and insecurity.* We are to open the door to our inner experience to the extent we can describe it. This level of relationship moves beyond *the trust of friendship* **to trusting in someone.** This means trusting that his or her deepest intentions are for our good. *Can we safely entrust everything about ourselves to him or her?* Trusting in someone *with good reason* is the proper foundation for entering a Covenant, either Marriage or the New Covenant.

After we enter a Covenant it is crucial that we continue to cultivate this level of openness, for our greatest growth, transformation, and intimacy require that we share our lives and hearts. Does this level of openness characterize your Marriage?

_____

All who worship images are put to shame...
PSALM 97:7

They became fools, and exchanged the glory of the immortal
God for images made to look like human beings...
ROMANS 1:22-23

THE WORLD'S APPROACH TO HONESTY AND OPENNESS

Let's consider the world's approach at this point, which is **image creation.** People devote much effort to creating an image in other's minds that will cause a favorable reaction. Meeting family or cultural expectations and covering up anything which would be viewed unfavorably has become an obsession in our day. We want to fit in, but to stand out. We want to be the best, have the best, dress the best and do the most amazing things; to be most influential, most beautiful, most powerful, most fit, most...whatever. Along the way, though, what about *who we really are*? What is really going on in our lives? Our society is characterized by loneliness, and loneliness is the direct result of hiding ourselves behind *our image.* Even if someone notices and responds to our image in the desired way, is this a response to *me*? Or to my success at subterfuge? To not be lonely we must be known and appreciated—loved, in fact—for who we are. How could that happen? Do you feel like anyone really knows you?

_____

_____

I, the Lord, search the heart and examine the mind, to reward a man according
to his conduct, according to what his deeds deserve.
JEREMIAH 17:10

God's plan is transparency. This is the opposite of hiding in plain sight behind an image. As we seek to develop transparency in our Marriage, keep in mind that our culture trains people to identify and exploit other's weaknesses on their path to supremacy. This level of openness is *only* safe and appropriate if one is building a relationship with someone *committed to love,* and *learning to love as God instructs.* All the rest of the elements on the "how we are to treat each other" list must also guide the two for transparency to be a sane strategy. If we are thinking of Marriage, what if we cannot safely entrust ourselves to our intended to this degree?

_____

_____

Why would God want us to be completely transparent in a Marriage? He wants us to be safe. He wants us to be secure. He wants us to able to trust the words of the other. He wants us to trust the intentions of the other. He wants us to be able to rely on the other for things large and small. He wants us to trust the motivations, the goals, the agendas, and the integrity of the other. Why? Because **such a relationship is the only place we can be real**. A place where our tender areas can be strengthened, our wounds healed, and our hidden potentials nurtured. In other words, the ground from which *every part of us* can grow, and the relationship can reach its full potential. Is your Marriage a safe and constructive place? Why or why not?

———————————————————————————————————————

———————————————————————————————————————

True intimacy—is the full sharing of life with another. It produces a certain *inner experience* of being loved, and a certain *shared experience of oneness*. These abundantly **fulfill our deepest need—to love and to be loved.** Have you been next to your husband or wife and experienced this oneness? It is overwhelming. It seems to take *us out of time*—as if we have always known each other and always will; it seems to transcend this realm—for it does. The fullness of love resides in the spiritual realm. This is what one-flesh *feels like*. Sexual intercourse often produces an experience akin to this, drawing from and celebrating the entire history of the couple. Then, physically depicting one being within the other—in the most pleasant and passionate way possible. God says to engage in intercourse frequently in Marriage. Can you think why this might be? What is your experience of intimacy?

———————————————————————————————————————

———————————————————————————————————————

Can you see God's step-by-step building plan in all of this? Factual accuracy of speech is the first step. If this is missing, can we even begin to build the rest? So it is with each step in this process. If a piece of this vital foundation is weak or missing, anything built atop it is unstable. Developing overall integrity is one of the key goals of Marriage. This outcome is worth any effort. How do we do this? One step at a time.

> *Search me, God, and know my heart; test me and know my anxious thoughts.*
> *See if there is any offensive way in me, and lead me in the way everlasting.*
> Psalm 139:23-24

God wants us to know ourselves instead of hiding. God wants us to know each other, instead of trading images. God wants us to refine the ways we treat each other, so we will be safe for each other, and assist each other in becoming the man or woman God intends us to be. **The first step on this journey is to be exceedingly careful about what we say and what we do.** Each step builds, and each step draws more and more from God's definition of love. At many points we must *review and revise our guidance system*, for our guidance system determines what we will do, despite our best intentions. **An unshakable commitment to faithfulness at every point** is the path to one step of growth after another. This will never be a straight-line, straightforward thing, nor will we get everything right—ever—on this earth. Holley and I still have occasional rough spots to work through. But now we know how to do this, and we have a huge toolbox of well-honed tools to work with. All I can tell you is that the results have been amazing so far, and keep getting better. What is your next step on the journey of your Marriage?

Our Marriage **feels like** a life of *passions lived out, an authentic expression of who we are* individually and as a couple. It feels like we have lots of ropes attached, all pulling in the same direction, urging us forward. It feels like we are walking at a strong pace down God's path, and He is pleased as we walk with Him. We have given Him our all, and have learned how to give more and more as we grow. Holley and I give our all to each other—which never looks like perfection, but does look like we are doing our best. And we have done better and better over time as we grow and grow together. God has given us all of this—life, life together in Him, and the universe we inhabit. We are living a one-flesh life. I would not want any other.

USING THE TOOLS GOD GAVE US

HOW DO WE DEVELOP THE ONE-FLESH LIFE WE HAVE BEEN GIVEN?

All Marriages are an exercise in damage control, rebuilding, and revision. *We hold on to what is good,* and turn what is not good into the motivation and resolve to grow. The biggest moves forward in Marriage and in life come from dealing with the biggest things that hold us back. So, do not be discouraged if your Marriage is far from perfect. Instead, be encouraged. You now have a curriculum for the near future for personal growth and Marriage improvement. Progress is slow—like one step after another on a long journey. Sometimes it seems progress is so slow that we will never get very far. But after months or years of slow and steady growth, look back. You will be amazed how much ground you have covered, and how many blessings have been added to your life and your Marriage. We build by using our three powers and God's Truth, with occasional direct guidance from God. Let us take a closer look at how we can use our own powers to fully cooperate with God, follow His plan and build the Marriage we want.

ASSENT AND DISSENT

We have absorbed a vast number of ideas about life and love from our culture. Only a few need to be reviewed and revised at any one time. How do we know what, and when? These ideas create problems. We can wait for trouble to come to us. But we must approach these troubles in a certain way—by looking for *our part* in the problem, even if this is not immediately obvious. When we are at odds with our spouse or with life itself we do well to consider the words of noted theologian Dierks Bentley: "I know what I was feeling, but what was I thinking?"[8] If something is not working it is not always about us. Other people contribute to most messes. But rather than taking a left turn into "only blame others," find something we can improve. How can we respond better or develop a more constructive viewpoint? Instead of asking, **"Why me?"** we do better to ask, **"Lord, what are you trying to teach me here?"** We should examine our thinking and our emotional response, as well as our goals, values, priorities, and other parts of our guidance system and ask one question: **"Why?"** If our reasoning is out of line with God's, now we know what to do next. Find God's truth. Then, we can follow the five-step plan to build truth into our daily lives that we saw in a previous chapter.

Conflict situations always involve either our guidance system or our character. Guidance system issues are about things that follow after the words, "I want ____." Character issues are about things that follow after the words, "I am ____." I don't know about you, but my mind has always been full of great ideas about life that do not come from God. I want this or that. But, why? Each of these ideas was sold to me at some point as a way to improve my life. I may not have acted on them yet; some may be in the "when I can" file. Others form my approach to life and other people. Yet, some of these—many in fact—are not in line with God. Which raises the eternal question: "Who do I believe, and to whom do I entrust my life?" Once I recognized a pattern in my mind—brushing past God to reach out for something that I was sure was a good idea—that is not in His plan for me, this changed everything. This is what Eve and Adam did. This move has been tried throughout history in innumerable lives. We may think what we get in this way is of some real benefit in the short run—sin "satisfies for a season"—but how about in the long run? Over sixty-plus years I am completely convinced that I know the answer, and so do you in the core of your being. Though we know the answer somewhere within, if we are to build the best Marriage we must take decisive action. We must clear up the confusion that keeps these ideas in our "OK for me" file. We must search out God's truth as if our lives depend on it. Because they do. Then, we must build this truth into our lives. Then, we must weed out competing ideas. These ideas show up in our inconsistencies and our conflicts, or when we are conflicted. What are the points of confusion in your life? What are you going to do about them?

_____

_____

Character issues and issues of *our perception of our identity* are covered in more detail in *The Covenant of Marriage*. These are trickier to spot, because these are things we simply assume are true of ourselves. We do not think about these things, we just live them. We live out to a degree *who we really are*, and we live out to a degree *who we think we are*. What if these are different? What if we are trying to be something we are not *because we concluded that this is who we are*. How satisfying a life is this? *Who we really are* is a being with certain potentials that must grow, develop, and mature. If we misunderstand who we are, how can we fully develop the being God made us to be? Therefore, we can seriously consider the way we fill in this blank: "I am ____." Many good things will come to mind, and should. But we may also find things like, "to blame for," "a loser," "always on the wrong side," "stupid, ugly, awkward," or many other unfavorable things. We are not perfect; we make mistakes; it is up to us to correct these things…but these do not define *who we are, made in the image of God*. Or, we may be "entitled to." Everyone, including God, may "owe me…;" "I deserve…" Is this really true? Once we fill in these blanks, we need to look at the Scriptures that tell us who God made us to be, who we are in Him, and who we are in our Marriage. Rather than living down to an incorrect view of ourselves, God has given us two remarkable opportunities: 1.) to be transformed by entry into a relationship with Him, and to be further transformed by entry into Marriage; 2.) to realize who we now are and build our new life—develop our potentials and grow to maturity. We cannot be whatever we want to be. We can do something better. We can become who we are. Who are you?

It helps if we develop the habit of looking at our behavior through the eyes of the recipient. In other words, **"What is it like to be on the other end of me?"** The question is simple: *"Is this a loving thing to do?"* There are many facets to love, so we may need to take some time to consider the question. If the answer is not apparent, a good followup would be: *"Is this the way I would like to be treated in this situation—why or why not?"* The third and most important question is, *"What does God's Word say about this matter?"* And if this is not clear, *"How do Covenant and my vows address this matter?"* The next time you have a conflict with your spouse, try this self-examination. Record what you find here:

_____

_____

ATTENTION

This is a wonderfully versatile and useful power. With it we make our spouse and Covenant the priorities they should be in our life. We have the power to refocus attention *from our spouse, or the problem to what is going on inside ourselves* in the middle of a conflict. Issues need to be resolved; but at the same time we cannot afford to miss a wonderful opportunity to grow. Would shifting our attention also shift *how we feel*? For me, it turns anger toward my wife and/or the situation into a search for hidden treasure. It is Holley's job to fix Holley, and my job to fix me. My best life is not found by fixing her, or having my way in the situation, but by fixing me. Would you rather fix your spouse, or fix yourself? Why?

_____

_____

In your next problem scenario, practice switching back and forth between two ideas: *"This is a disaster,"* and *"This is an opportunity to learn and grow."* As you shift between these two, **notice your feelings**. Do you feel anxiety with one focus, and gratitude and peace with the other? When facing problems it is remarkably helpful to "make our request known to God," and to find *something to thank God for* about the situation (Philippians 4:6-7). It is helpful to "reframe" the situation into its least destructive and disruptive form. Does this issue perhaps mean the end of life as I know it, or will I not really care how this turns out by the end of the week? Few issues are truly a hill to die on. If we are facing a serious threat it is helpful to look squarely at the worst-case scenario. Then, consider how to deal with it instead of remaining paralyzed by fear. In every situation we benefit greatly from directing our thoughts to the most helpful perspective. Why? Because our feeling will follow. Many people would say, "We can't change how we feel." Do you agree?

_____

_____

The power of attention orders our day, sets every priority and value, and charts the course of our life by determining what is most important for us. We generally focus on only one thing at a time. We are often unaware of other considerations in the moment. We may be unaware we are considering a decision that violates God's moral universe, and we are about to multiply our problems. We may face an issue unaware that, in Covenant with God, we have access to His literally unlimited resources—which He will entrust to us in ways that most benefit us. We looked at fingers or the wall behind them, but we can train ourselves to keep both in view. Instead of keeping God and spiritual realities in view, or a physical reality that is full of problems, we want to develop the ability to become "co-conscious," fully aware of both realms at once. We always want to have spiritual realities in view when we make any decision. We can choose to see the best in a friend or listen to slander. We can choose to focus on our limitations, or on finding out what God wants to do through us. We can see ourselves as we always have, or realize that, in Covenant, we have been made new and different. We can keep living "our" life, or realize we are called to a different life. Many people have not consciously developed the power to shift from a less beneficial view to a more beneficial one. But with practice this important power can direct us to an enjoyable life, balanced emotions, and better relationships. What uses can you think of for a stronger power of attention in your life?

INTENTION

How committed are we to complete a task? "Good intentions" are often code for a weak power of intention. This implies we *intended one thing but did something else.* In fact, **we do what we intend—always.** If we *did not* do it, we never really intended to in this circumstance. This is not to say that we always intend words or actions to have the impact they have (that is a different question, one which depends on the receiver as well as the sender). With a well-developed power of intention we complete necessary and important tasks. We become capable of overcoming any circumstance standing in the way of doing what is right, good, true, loving, and faithful.

People devote vast time and energy to physical fitness. Developing our power of intention is much the same process. Start with smaller commitments. Practice overcoming smaller obstacles. Do not expect perfection initially. We need to *learn how* to achieve larger things. Few can walk into a gym and design the perfect workout for themselves. To succeed, people study fitness, seek coaching, and also work on related things like diet and sleep. Building our willpower requires that we continue to build every part of our character. Seek help and advice from mature Christians. The thing we need most is ***a reason*** to grow and develop *this power*. One good reason: *this power determines the extent of our overall growth and development.* Look into the eyes of your beloved and ask yourself what you are willing to do to become the best lover, friend, and Covenant partner for this person. What reasons do you have to strengthen this power in your Marriage?

Is a picture of God's Covenant plan beginning to form in your mind? 1. Our transformation and joining. 2. Recognizing our new identity and bond, and *embracing* the realities of this relationship. 3. Learning what *love in action* is by experiencing God's love for us; and by learning His injunctions to us in Scripture and faithfulness to our Covenant—two sides of the same coin. 4. Transforming our minds into accord with these truths—our guidance system, our character, our perception of our identity. But why should we go to the trouble do all of these things?

LESSON TEN

BUILDING LOVE FOR A LIFETIME and COVENANT VERSUS CONTRACT

...A CRUCIAL DISTINCTION

Why did you get married? *Because you are in love with someone.* You want to share your lives and do life together. You could not imagine not being together for the rest of your lives. Love is a magnetic force that pulls two together. Covenant is the bond that joins two together. But, what holds people together for a lifetime? How can two *grow their love over a lifetime*? If we look around, we see many different plans in action. Everyone is convinced they found the right person and the right plan. But what happens next? As the fine print says, "Results may vary." Everyone is equally married, but all marriages are not equal. Why?

From the beginning Holley and I have been very competitive in a wonderful way. The attraction we felt toward each other was delightful. That someone cared about us in general was wonderful. But our energy was directed toward understanding each other, so we could do things for each other that would be a blessing. Then, we tried to out-bless each other. There is nothing unusual about this. What is perhaps unusual is that this pattern never stopped. Is it unusual that our hearts are more on fire for each other decades into our relationship than they were in the beginning? Several times a year a stranger will come up to us in a public place and ask how long we have been together. They are always amazed at our answer. There is apparently something about our love that is palpable across a room, and unusual enough to deserve comment. People assume we are just falling in love. I suppose we still are. Our relationship had a great beginning, as many do. But why did it continue to get better?

What determines how two people feel about each other two or ten or forty years into a Marriage? Some stay best friends. Their friendship deepens. They become for each other part of the answer to the problems of life. Or, people stay together but walk apart. Best friends turn into something else. Instead of the answer, spouses can become the problem. Sometimes a problem so big that people walk away. Was this not the right person? Was it not true love after all? Is true love found, or built? What do you think?

The wise woman builds her house, but with her own hands the foolish one tears hers down.
Proverbs 14:1

How we feel about each other over time is mostly about how we are treated. What is their attitude toward us? What place do we occupy in his or her life? **Do you see what God wants to do here through Covenant?** Covenant is about faithfulness to…what? To things that build the best relationship. To things that build the deepest love. To things that build the best experience for both. To things that create a home where each person can grow the new being they have become to maturity and develop unrecognized potentials. A place of refuge and healing, a place of love and joy. A place filled with the blessings of God. Covenant is about growing our love for each other by *growing us*. This is what Marriage can be. Our choices determine whether it becomes this. Do we build with both hands, or build with one as we tear down with the other?

What is the other plan, the world's plan? Be yourself. That is, be what you think you are supposed to be according to the world. Go after things the world tells you are important. And who is most important? If you found the right person and true love, this person will *love you as you are*, expect nothing more of you, and deal with whatever damage you inflict on them. Isn't this what true love means? People expect true love, unconditional love, but what do they offer in return? People are trained to think they have a right to do what they feel like. Don't settle, don't give in. Is this a working plan? Why or why not?

God's answer is Covenant—join and transform. Then, do life together. Realize you are an extension of each other and treat each other in this way. Make each other the most important thing in your life (other than God), and keep each other in this position no matter what. Love, protect, and provide for the other as for yourself. Embrace God's plan to inform, conform, and transform. Learn *what true love looks like*. Conform to all the things God tells us to do and Covenant tells us to do that are love in action. Do your best to love, then use the tools God built into you and into this relationship to grow.

We all do well in the beginning because our hearts are on fire for each other…in the beginning. Then, things return to…what? To the ways we have always treated other people? To the place we assign important people in our lives, versus all the other things in life we think are important? To our habits, our character, our view of ourselves, our view of what life is supposed to be? Do we live out our view of what Marriage is supposed to be? What is God's plan to *meet us where we are and move us where He wants us to be?* Our new life and bond, the issues of life (which bring to our attention our need to change), our powers coupled with His truth under the direction of His Spirit (to transform our minds, then everything else within us). God's plan is there, waiting for us to take hold of it. **What, then, determines the outcome of our Marriage?** Our decisions. What new decisions could you make that will improve your Marriage?

As we look at a person next to us, part of our loving feelings have to do with our respect for them. We are to honor, but *what is the person like* that we try to honor? We naturally admire people who have many virtues. If integrity, wisdom, kindness, and all the other elements of character and behavior that God calls good are part of someone's life, or, if they are seriously trying to build these things into their life, respect is earned. What does God's Covenant plan invite us to do? To develop these very attributes. It is building these things into our lives that allows us to love *more deeply in more ways.* When we adjust our guidance system and revise our character, we are building these attributes within ourselves. How has personal growth built more love in your Marriage?

The big picture: God wants certain things to be added to our lives and subtracted from our lives. Why? So we can build the best relationship, experience the deepest love, and become the best version of ourselves, among other reasons. Really, it is because **He loves us and wants the best for us.** We must never lose sight of these ultimate truths about our life and God's love. God wants us to build things into our lives that build good things. He wants us to remove things we embraced because we *thought they were true* about life, love, and ourselves—that do real damage. It is really that simple.

We have talked a lot about love-in-action—about loving the other. A lifetime love affair also means that our hearts must feel love more and more deeply. Isn't this what we want most of all? How does this happen? Several moving parts go together to form the experience of love. God's Covenant plan touches them all. First, we fell in love with our spouse. Our hearts deem this person worth loving with our whole heart. But close relationships also frustrate, wound, and disappoint. Fortunately, perfection is not necessary. But, what is necessary? Another part of love is how we choose to view another, and how much of an investment we choose to make in them. Love is a response, but it is also a choice. How are we to view each other in Covenant? What kind of investment is called for by Covenant? What does it mean to make a choice to love?

Now to Him who is able to do immeasurably more than all we ask or imagine,
according to His power that is at work within us...
Ephesians 3:20

Another part of love is *being part of something bigger than ourselves that is building something worthwhile.* Early on we dream of what life would be like together. As Holley and I live out God's plan we are continually amazed at what has been built, and what is being built in and through our lives. We would be delighted with a fraction of these things. **God's plans were far beyond our imagination.** Has this all been fun and games? Not at all. We have had a full share of trails and struggles. But we followed God's plan going through these things as best we knew how. We continued to search out His plan and adjust things in ourselves. We held on to Him more tightly and learned from Him. Even the hardest things in our lives were important building blocks. Two of the most reassuring lessons in all of life are coming to understand that God will never leave us or forsake us (Matthew 28:20), and that all things work together for those who love God and are called according to His purposes (Romans 8:28). We can trust His plan, and trust in Him. How has adversity built important things in your Marriage?

Another part of the experience of love is being wholehearted. **Can you or I feel overflowing love if we are conflicted or confused?** There are lots of pieces to this one! Some of this is about the other person's heart, character, and behavior. Confusion and inner conflict may be a red flag about the other person. But another part may be about us. Have we been wounded, and do we now refuse to trust? There are myriad reasons we may not wholeheartedly offer ourselves even when we have every reason to do so. Many people sabotage a relationship when someone is getting "too close" instead of identifying and dealing with their own wrong conclusions. It is true to say "someone…" It is not true to say, "Therefore, everyone…" We should not be rigidly pessimistic or foolishly optimistic—instead, **God wants us to be discerning and realistic.** As always, we must seek out the deception that drives the dysfunction, then seek the truth. Then, use our power of assent and dissent to replace the lie with truth.

We will not always feel the love even when we are loved. Many ideas about ourselves, others, or life may need revision over the course of our life. The key—when we are unhappy, frustrated, or in pain—is *not to expect our spouse to fix this and blame them if they do not.* The key is to approach our heart issues first with a question: "What am I thinking?" Are our thoughts in line with God and reality? Or, are we living out a deception? This is how deception *feels*—pain, anger, frustration, confusion. Like we are trapped in a dark place. But, we hold the key—one given to us by God. *Be transformed by the renewing of your mind…* (Romans 12:2).

God's Covenant plan is designed to fill our hearts and our lives with love. Consider Jesus. Look at the ways people reacted to Him and His circumstances. He was troubled on occasion, but never off-balance. He dealt with deception in literally *everyone* around Him—by speaking the truth in love—and never lost sight of His proper role. He was never defined by circumstances or devastated by circumstances. He represented God faithfully in the midst of circumstances. The word "Christian" literally means "Little Christ." What guidance does this offer for your Marriage?

Think of the best Marriage you have seen up close. How many elements of Covenant are lived out in this relationship? If you were fortunate enough to have parents with a great Marriage, you got to see some of the inner workings. Many are not so fortunate; many have never seen a great Marriage up close. People may admire two people in a lifelong Marital love affair, but have no idea what went into building it. We have tried to lay out a blueprint in the detail this study will allow.

Now, think of a Marriage you have seen up close that is struggling. How many elements of Covenant are missing from this relationship? But, notice something else. Notice not just the absence of Covenant elements, but the *presence* of a different plan. I want to briefly illustrate this plan, for all of us have been influenced by it. These are the ideas about Marriage that fill our culture. This is the world's plan: a contract. Since this approach leads us in a completely different direction from Covenant, we want to be sure we do not have one foot on each path. Unfortunately, the world's concept of Marriage has also found its way into the Christian community and Christian teaching. What problems are created by viewing Marriage as a contract?

COVENANT VERSUS CONTRACT

A contract is **an agreement between two separate and distinct entities.** No one makes a contract with themselves. A contract *lists what the parties will do and will not do. A contract defines behavior—period. A contract is entered with one ultimate motivation—self interest.* One offers something, but intends to receive something of greater perceived value. Contracts cover a *limited list of behaviors.* Anything *not on the list is not a part of the deal.* Contracts are *held together by agreement.* Remaining in this arrangement requires **ongoing agreement that can be withdrawn at any time if the other party fails to live up to the contract's terms**—one's perception. What is the difference between this plan and Covenant?

THE CONTRACTUAL MODEL CREATES THE "COMPETING KINGDOMS" MODEL

Contracts are made between *two separate and distinct entities,* separate lives held together only by *agreement.* Thus, Marriage becomes **a Kingdom and a Queendom.** The two rule over separate realms—*their lives.* I refer to this as *the Competing Kingdoms Model of Marriage.* If one is not consciously living out a Covenant model of Marriage, *this is literally the only other option.*

If we **are not aware** that *our identity has changed and is now joined to another* when we enter Marriage, **how do we view ourselves?** In the same way we always have. We spent our lives building what? *Our own* *lives.* We want Marriage to be what? Value added to our lives. How do we build the life we want, according to our culture? *By getting our way*: having things how we want them, pursuing our preferences, satisfying our needs, and gratifying our desires. We are a monarch who deeply desires to be in charge of as much as possible, because **enlarging our influence equals a better life.** Thanks to our culture most believe this is the path to true happiness. Is this actually true? But this is the starting point in Marriage for most people, even if they are head-over-heels in love. Does this model describe many Marriages? Does it describe yours?

THE COMPETING KINGDOMS MODEL CREATES AN INTERNAL CONFLICT

Our beloved is **still a completely separate person**. So now, we have the dilemma of *balancing our good intentions* toward this other person *with our perception of our best interests*. In practice, this leads to competing priorities within each party as he or she tries to juggle good intentions versus personal interests. It also results in sharply competing priorities *between* the parties. Why? The other person is doing the same juggling act, calculating how much they want to give, or give up, to get what they want. The bottom line? **Each wants to come out on top.** There is a deep root of conflict here: a willingness to sacrifice relationship to get the "win" versus goodwill and the desire to build the relationship. *The rest of this dance is figuring out who is going to do the sacrificing and who gets his or her way in each scenario.* Have you been in a competition-based relationship? What did it feel like?

If people pursue self-interest at the expense of the relationship, what happens to the relationship? *Poor treatment damages hearts and relationships, and a wedding ring does not alter this reality.* In fact, *the Covenant violation* of such treatment is yet another offense that registers in the heart. Even if these people genuinely like each other you still see people undercutting each other, **trying to neuter each other to alter the balance of power.** Why? Because **the more power the other person has, the less apt one is to get one's own way.** And, after all, isn't this really the path to our own happiness? How do outpourings of hostility and disrespect from someone who "loves" us impact our experience of Marriage?

THE COMPETING KINGDOMS MODEL WITH A CHRISTIAN VENEER

Even if we overlay Christian principles and beliefs, we see the same jousting match and the same results. Christians may have additional relationship skills. They may pursue their interests with less obvious aggression. And there is a train of thought in the Christian community that we are supposed to be sacrificial, to lay down our own desires, feelings, agenda, and will for the sake of God and each other. But these only partially mitigate damage inflicted by two people who believe they are pursuing separate lives side-by-side. We have seen how conflict is conducted within the Covenant model. In the winner-take-all contractual model, even between Christians conflicts can go very wrong. How would you explain the difference in the way conflict is handled in these two models?

_____

_____

Are there any ways you conduct your Marriage like a contract?

_____

_____

.

...choose for yourselves this day whom you will serve.
But for me and my household, we will serve the Lord.
JOSHUA 24:15

WHICH MODEL WILL YOU CHOOSE?

If we affirm the reality of Marriage we may still draw heavily from the contractual side because this is all we have ever seen. The contractual model and its consequences are described so we can notice these things in our Marriage and take steps to adjust. How could you adjust your approach?

_____

_____

_____

_____

Do not merely look out for your own interests, but also for the interests of others.
PHILIPPIANS 2:4

SELFLESSNESS AND SELFISHNESS

In Marriage between Christians there is another pitfall: a particular view of "personal sacrifice" as a virtue, and as *the definition of love*. This is a virtue if the nature of the sacrifice is correctly defined. Love does involve sacrifice at times. Instead, we are taught a dichotomy—selflessness vs. selfishness. The former is supposedly a Godly approach, the latter is the definition of bad. There is an element of truth in this view, but we must be very careful. The term "selfless" does not appear in Scripture. What we do see is the need to properly balance our needs and the needs of others. Our needs are not more important than others, but are they less important? Is the abundant life about meeting our true needs, or learning to completely overlook them? Did God build needs within us to be ignored? **This view could not be more in conflict with the mutual love-in-action of Covenant.** There is an asterisk here. At times God must challenge our guidance system's *incorrect perception of our needs*. He may need to show us our true needs, or remind us that He ultimately meets all our needs. Even if God is taking corrective action, this is *still about meeting our deepest needs*. This is still about loving us in the ways we need most. In Marriage we are not to think more highly of ourselves than we ought, nor are we to think less than we should of a creature made in God's image, even if this creature is ourselves. Has God shown you how much He truly values you?

Do you feel valued by your spouse? How valuable is he or she in your eyes?

To love someone is never to say that their needs do not matter. Why do we stress this? Because focusing *only on others* does not solve a problem for us, it actually creates a problem.

We love because He first loved us.
I JOHN 4:19

We seem to be only capable of **knowing another** to the depth that we *know ourselves*. We seem to only be capable of **loving another** to the depth that we love ourselves. God's first directive is to love another *as we love ourselves*. So, does God want us to **love ourselves more**? Consider His definition of love. We love because **He first loved us**. We must be loved, and learn what God's love means by experience before we can display this love to others. Do we ignore our real needs as we scurry around meeting the needs (or wants, or demands) of others? If so, this keeps us from developing the ability to love deeply. Have you ever considered seeking to experience more of God's love? *Have you considered* learning to love yourself more—*so you can love your spouse more?*

SELFLESSNESS = CO-DEPENDENCY?

The belief that our needs exist to be ignored and we exist only to meet the needs of others can progress to co-dependency. Here, *another agrees that we exist only to meet his or her needs.* There is *nothing mutual,* **no reciprocity**. We exist to implement his or her agenda, to aid and abet his or her selfishness. Many Christians dutifully pursue this course, "loving" the other, waiting for him or her to be changed by this "love." Yet, such "love offerings" lead to more demands and more disrespect. Covenant says love within Marriage is the most mutual of all things. Anything less violates the very heart of Covenant—God's definition of love. Those who find themselves in such a relationship benefit from finding a good Christian counselor. Prying the controlling hand of another off of one's life is a challenging and lengthy process. First, we must realize that *continuing to build this dysfunctional pattern* is not loving *toward self,* nor is it a display of love toward the one we are trying to love. Love is always based on truth. This pattern violates the truth of Marriage.

IF YOUR MARRIAGE PARTNER'S APPROACH IS NOT COVENANTAL

"For I know the plans I have for you," declares the Lord. "Plans to prosper you and not to harm you, plans to give you hope and a future.,"
Jeremiah 29:11

Do not be yoked together with unbelievers...
2 Corinthians 6:14

There is not a single or simple answer to this question. The person may be a non-Christian, or a Christian who has not embraced this part of God's plan. We all embrace ideas from many sources to form our approach to life. These ideas may be correct, or wildly incorrect. Still, this is *a person's truth.* The door someone must go through to *change an embraced truth* has a handle only on the inside. It is always a good idea to speak the truth in love—to share what is true and what this truth means to you. If your spouse is willing to go through this guidebook with you or read *The Covenant of Marriage,* you are dealing with someone who is open to new views and willing to learn. Changing a view of Marriage is much like changing one's view of God. **Look at the exchanges Jesus had with people.** He spoke truths straight from the mouth of God. Yet, people responded in many ways. Some walked away, some stayed to hear more, some left everything to follow Him. Jesus spoke truth and lived truth. His life demonstrated the power of truth and a character in harmony truth. But He—God—let people draw their own conclusions and did not apply additional coercion. He was patient. He prayed. Perhaps this is our best model. God has ways of getting a person's attention and opening eyes. Pray for this.

PRAYER

Prayer moves God to unlock reluctant hearts, to break down strongholds, and to lead people to His way (not to our way, by the way). Yet, such change, if it comes, may not be on the timetable we desire. We often have much to learn about God and life as we struggle through unwelcome situations. Time with God in prayer is not just about moving God to solve a problem; it is about building our relationship with Him and allowing Him to build us as we go through challenges. Sometimes, God must be enough for us. If we are in Covenant with Him, His incredible heart and mighty power are there to love us, even if our spouse is not there for us.

BE FAITHFUL YOURSELF

Your own faithfulness to Covenant is vital for several reasons. This shows your spouse the real benefits of this approach. Even if he or she does not respond as desired, you grow. Your outer life grows and transforms. You develop new perspective, new skills, new insight, new capabilities. You can better handle whatever you encounter. We have certainly had experience with asymmetric relationships—loving someone, but having something very different coming back to us. This is painful and impacts us in many ways. God values faithfulness to Him in any situation, including ones that are devastating. He will **protect and reward us** if we are in His school of love and life. Perhaps not in the ways we would like, but in **the ways we most need.** We are all on a journey that takes us places we never anticipated—sometimes to places we would not choose to go. **God uses these difficult times**—in fact, especially uses these difficult times. He grows things within us necessary for the rest of the life He has planned for us. **Paul learned a great secret: being content in every circumstance.** This is a wonderful model for dealing with a Marriage that is less than God intends it to be, and much less than our hearts yearn for.

If possible, so far as it depends on you, be at peace with all men.
Romans 12:18 (NASB)

My peace I give you. Do not let your hearts be troubled and do not be afraid.
John 14:27

Remember, we are here for only a short time—passing through on the way to eternity. What we do while we are here has great impact on our eternity. At the same time, *we are not responsible for fixing every problem in our sphere—including our Marriage.* **We cannot make another follow God or build a better Marriage;** neither can another **make us be unfaithful or damage our relationship with God.** We are to protect ourselves: if abused, one should involve professional third parties or the authorities. Sometimes the one we never thought would change turns to God. Or, the prodigal never returns. God allows each of us to embrace the truths we choose. The truths we choose form us, but also reveal something about us. We must allow others the same freedom God allows us—to select the course of our lives, in this life and for eternity. Regardless of what another chooses, if we are in Covenant with God we are joined to a loving Father who will never leave or forsake us. Life is long, and our story is not finished yet.

LESSON ELEVEN

PUTTING IT ALL TOGETHER and A FEW MORE KEY ELEMENTS

For the Lord gives wisdom; from His mouth come knowledge and understanding.
He holds success in store for the upright, He is a shield for those whose walk is blameless,
for He guards the course of the just and protects the way of His faithful ones.
PROVERBS 2:6-8

In stark contrast to a contract, Marriage **forges the most powerful possible connection**. We **cannot fully perceive** this joining or the transformation this merger creates within us. But, if we walk by faith and not by sight—if we build the relationship *upon these realities*—amazing things happen. Everything God says to do *builds a better Marriage*. This may be different from the way we have ever treated someone. These new ways may feel awkward at first. Soon, though, they will feel *authentic*—like what we wanted to do all along, we just did not realize it. **Loving our husband or wife is our new native tongue**, the most satisfying thing we can do for them and for ourselves. It is more blessed to give than to receive. These blessings compound going forward. Following His plan we build a certain quality of relationship, a true home. A place where we feel safe enough to *be ourselves*—honest and transparent. A relationship in which we *enjoy the delights of intimacy and love that continue to grow*. This openness and acceptance is the ground from which unrecognized potentials can be nurtured. We can become the person God created us to be. God does have a plan.

We saw a snapshot of the building process. It would take a lifetime to fully explore this plan even for one life, much less for every life (fortunately, you have lifetime to explore it for your own life). Yet, this same plan applies to every person, Marriage, and life situation throughout history. This is miraculous. How is that possible? Only God…

…wisdom calls aloud…, "the waywardness of the simple will kill them, and the complacency of fools will destroy them; but whoever listens to me will live in safety and be at ease, without fear of harm."
PROVERBS 1:20, 32-33

IS THERE A SHORTCUT TO GLORY?

God's plan is all about wisdom, **about things which yield the best long-term results.** It is amazing how susceptible we humans are to a sales pitch *to take a shortcut to glory*—that does not actually exist. Suppose someone offered you two choices: a million dollars for one night, but every trace of the money and what you did with it would be gone the next morning; or financial resources that would meet your needs for the rest of your life—on the condition that you carefully follow a plan to use these resources. Which would you choose? **People seek intimacy and connection** in "casual" sex, though there is no such thing. Intercourse creates a Covenant, creating a bond and altering identity, whether or not it is recognized or honored. This is why God notes that sexual sin damages us in a unique way (I Corinthians 6:18). Or, **people want love-for-a-lifetime**, but never understand their role in building this kind of relationship. So, he or she tries to build a lifetime relationship with behavior which exhausts the mate's coping mechanisms. God's plan is total commitment, slow growth, ultimate gratification and fulfillment beyond our dreams. Do you think there is another path to the same fulfillment God offers? What is it?

TAKING THE LONG VIEW

We **tend to take an in-the-moment view of relationship.** Is the person still mad at me, or did he or she get over it and now we're OK again? What can I say that will make them start talking to me again? I know, I'll say, "I'm sorry…" As long as someone *comes back to us* with an open heart and open arms **we believe it is a win**. And we can resume business as usual. We tend to overlook our behavior, and how much damage we did to heart and relationship. God's rule is *unremitting* faithfulness, *consistent* love, and *building with both hands*—**always.** Why is this so extreme? Because **God sees every consequence of behavior from beginning to end.** He sees the long-term damage. Perhaps more important, if people are in this damage-and-make-up pattern, even though the relationship has survived (at least to this point) it is *not growing into what it can become.* **God's concern is the lost opportunity to build what could be.** We tend only to look at the delights of the present moment, or their absence. God's plan is to build something over time that is far bigger, deeper, broader, and more powerful than anything we could have in the short term. **Consistency is the key to this outcome.** This is why **Covenant is laced together with the highest level of commitment possible.** Not just the bond which defines this relationship, but a commitment to the behaviors and attitudes which consistently live out this reality. Do you think this kind of consistency can happen in the real world? How? Or, why not?

REBUILDING A SHAKY FOUNDATION

If one lies to avoid a problem scenario or create a better image, or for any other reason, one trains the other to doubt one's words. We term this a "trust issue," but **do we understand its remarkably serious consequences?** If we cannot even trust the words coming out of a person's mouth, what else are they concealing? If reality is replaced by manipulation—in what other situations will we discover this? How do we know when to believe, and when we are being played? How can we be sure of the person's true heart toward us? If we cannot reasonably trust the words, how can we *trust in* this person—and open our life and heart to the care of this person? We may already be married. The relationship may exist, but the many elements which build love-for-a-lifetime cannot grow in an environment of mistrust.

The solution is to begin where we are in the process. First, we must pay careful attention to **every word** that comes out of our mouths, and careful attention to follow through to **do everything we say we will do**. Upon this foundation more can be built.

Trust can be regained. But not by just saying we're sorry. **Trust can be regained by genuine repentance.** Repentance means *coming to understand the impact of behavior on the other*—**seeing this situation through their eyes and through God's eyes.** Then renouncing—not just the *event—but the pattern of behavior and the ideas upon which it is founded.* It helps to envision a mistake not as a single event, but as walking in one direction or another. People never commit one act of disobedience. They always commit many. One false move leads inevitably to another. Why? Disobedience is a path we choose, rather than an act. The word "repentance" literally means to turn 180° and walk in the opposite direction. Do you see why this term is used? Repentance means to turn *and commit oneself to walking God's path.*

That is, for this issue we *develop a new guidance system* based on God's Word using the same five step process detailed in the previous lesson. The level of trust needed to *build relationship* cannot be rebuilt until the person has developed—then **lived out—a new conviction**. It may take awhile for the other to trust, depending on the magnitude of the damage. Again, **the desired endpoint is not the other party ceasing to turn away from us; it is resuming growth in the relationship based on full trust and confidence**. Have you seen trust rebuilt in a relationship? How did this happen?

_____

_____

This illustrates what it takes to rebuild one foundation stone of a Marriage. This same process can be applied to any other part of Marriage. What foundation stones of your Marriage—trust, respect, commitment—need to be revised?

_____

_____

A FEW MORE KEY ELEMENTS

There are a large number of elements we could discuss here. Do not be limited by the ones we choose. Add your own relationship and life lessons to this list and discuss these with your husband or wife. Here is a sampling of things Holley and Mark have found to be very important in their lives and Marriage.

Submit to one another out of reverence for Christ.
Ephesians 5:21

SUBMISSION

We speak in *The Covenant of Marriage* at length about this often-misunderstood topic. **A parody of submission has become a lightening rod in our culture**. To understand the real thing, envision two people who are CEO and COO of a company. To make the best decisions for the company, each has *laid aside* the imperative of ramming through their own agenda. Each has *taken up* the imperative of finding the best course for the company (which is also best for both parties). Then, add the imperatives of following God's Word and His path, and loving each other as God loves us. Working out differences is about *getting it right* for both. We must recognize, and occasionally defer to, the real needs or agenda of the other. **But Holley and I find in practice that we often end up with a solution neither of us brought to the table.** God directs us to an even better course as we thoroughly examine circumstance, minds and hearts, and seek His will for our family and our lives. This is taking the long view instead of seeking the joy of an in-the-moment win—which compromises something important in the long run. Submission is first of all a mutual thing, as is everything else in Covenant.

Wives, submit to your own husbands as you do to the Lord.
Ephesians 5:22

Husbands, love you wives just as Christ loved the church...
Ephesians 5:25

Humans, reflecting the nature of Eve and Adam's new buddy in the Garden of Eden, want to **step out of the God-created order** and push their way to the top, creating a new order of importance in the universe—**with self at the top**. Submission accepts God's reality check on this point. God put in place an administrative hierarchy in the case of a deadlock—the husband gets the call. But **the husband is not at the top** of this hierarchy. **God is.** God's order does not work unless He is directing it. In every human institution someone is designated to make the final call. This is not necessarily the most capable person. *Nor is this a statement about the relative value of two people—which it is often taken to be.* It is the way to get a decision made and move on. Even if one fully understands God's plan, though, submission is not always easy. See Jesus's discussion with His Father in the Garden of Gethsemane for details. It is even more difficult for a person to submit to another human, especially when convinced she is right on an important issue. The ultimate issue, though, is whom we trust the most. What is your view of submission?

_____

_____

LOVE LANGUAGES

Misunderstandings can be more than a male-female thing. Gary Chapman has done the world a great service by writing a series of books on Love Languages[9]. This is a wonderful starting point, directing us away from **loving the other in our language to loving them in their language**, the one they can hear and feel. We must learn to do things that create the experience of _being loved_ in the heart of our beloved. If we do something and it falls flat or sends the wrong message, this is not a rejection of you or your love. This is a love-language issue. You are speaking to them in Chinese. **Have a good laugh, shake it off, listen, learn, adjust, adapt, and prevail.** What have you done for the sake of love…that fell flat?

_____

_____

OUR DEEPEST EMOTIONAL NEEDS

One of the adventures of the first year or ten of Marriage is figuring out what the other person really wants and needs—and figuring out what you really want and need. Part of our uniqueness is having **a unique combination of needs.** There are perhaps twenty different core needs—deepest emotional needs—a person might have. Any individual will have three or four that are most important to them. It is extremely helpful to know our own and our spouse's—this will narrow the search when we are looking for the most special ways to say, "I love you!" Some people like to be touched, other do not. Some like to share, others prefer to listen. Some like acts of service, others crave quality time, prefer a gift or perhaps an affirming and encouraging word. At the outset, many people do not know their deepest needs. Part of our need-meeting duty in Covenant is to discern—then meet—our partner's deepest needs, and help them meet ours. A couple's core needs may or may not overlap. How do we determine what these are? We must study our spouse's responses. We must learn to read between the lines. We are always looking for things that are particularly significant to them, that impact them greatly. Over time you will see whether or not encouragement really matters, and if not, what does matter. Here is a tip: look carefully for **what someone likes** most, and **what hurts** them the most. What are your core needs, and your spouse's?

_____

_____

THE IMPORTANCE OF ASKING

In the same vein, an important relationship tool is **asking for what we need. Guessing games are fun… for a while**. Part of honesty and transparency is to react honestly. We need to *reveal to our Covenant partner the things which really matter to us*. Need-meeting is a learning curve for giver and receiver. One of the best gifts we can give is to **be clear about what we need,** what we **do not want,** and **what is painful** for us. This helps our beloved focus his or her efforts. No one likes to make a significant effort for another that is met with a blank face or a dismissive word.

There is an important flip-side to asking, however. It is important to ask, but we must also offer another element of love—**the freedom to respond, or not**. Our partner may not be able to meet our need or fulfill our request in a given moment. A request is simply that: a request. We need to offer the freedom to meet a need, or graciously accept a "no" or an "I'll get back to you on that one." *This removes the dynamic of manipulation or coercion from the equation.* **If someone loves us they will find a way, when he or she can, to do important things for us.** The question is timing. Or, perhaps our partner differs with us about what is truly best. The realm of needs is wonderful to explore together. It is also vital to **remember Who is ultimately tasked with meeting our true needs—God.** Our spouse is *not* our primary source of need-meeting, though God may use them in this capacity much of the time. If our mindset is, "I need this and I need it right now," we need to have this conversation with God. What happens in your Marriage when the answer is "no," or "later?"

Consider it pure joy, my brothers and sisters, whenever you face trials…because you know that the testing of your faith produces perseverance. Let perseverance finish its work so that you may be mature and complete, not lacking anything.

JAMES 1:2

THE PURPOSE OF ADVERSITY AND PAIN

We enter Marriage seeking bliss and delight. Unfortunately, even the most blessed life is not a steady diet of pleasant experiences. Life is more like a balanced diet, from the ridiculous to the sublime, the worst to the most divine. Adversity, pain, and loss **can wreck a life or a relationship**. Or, the same circumstances **can produce maturity, resolve, a deeper capacity to love, and a stronger and more resilient Marriage**. What is the difference between these two? *What we believe* about certain things, and *how we live* as a result of these beliefs.

We each have a measuring stick that we hold up against every circumstance. This stick is calibrated according to the way we understand our self-interest. If we think a circumstance *advances* our self-interest, **it is good.** If it *threatens something we think is important*, the circumstance is **bad.** If it threatens something *we deem vitally important*, the circumstance is **horrible.** When a circumstance measures bad, or worse, **what goes on inside us?** We become anxious, fearful, threatened, insecure. This issue preoccupies us. **It**

takes over our life and impacts our relationships. We *desperately need* a certain outcome. But, perhaps this outcome is not what happens. At this point we are most apt to question God's love. Have you ever faced a crisis of faith because of a loss?

———————————————————————————————————

———————————————————————————————————

How did you resolve this crisis?

———————————————————————————————————

———————————————————————————————————

Holley and Mark have noticed something over the decades. We have had some worst-case-scenario outcomes—experiencing serious damage, deep loss and significant pain. However, over time these **terrible things** proved to be the foundation for some of the **best and most important things** God wanted to build into our lives and our Marriage. **So, were these things good, or bad?** Painful, yes. But bad? In the moment, they certainly appeared to be. *But God is about the long term, about building, about ending up with something truly worth having.* At times He needs to strip things away, perhaps very painfully, *to prepare the way for something better.* At times we need to let go of something *we think is vital,* because God wants a better life for us based on different things. He may need to pry our hands off an idol. We may need to be left with only God, to discover that *He is truly sufficient for us.* **If we have Him and nothing else, it is enough; if we have everything else, but not Him, it is never enough.** We must learn to trust His love even when serious loss occurs. For this is not the end of our story. Have you experienced your own 'rest of the story'?

———————————————————————————————————

———————————————————————————————————

God knows what we need. We often do not. We can safely allow Him to make the call about what is best even if we do not understand why at the time. *What does this shift in perspective do?* It keeps us from being anxious in troubled waters. It keeps us from **having our eyes taken off what God wants us to be doing**—and instead *riveted to our worries and fears.* **It replaces anxiety with trust and peace,** as it says in Philippians 4:8-9. This in turn allows us to face the most threatening circumstances **with peace in our hearts and a smile on our faces** that is genuine, for we are confident in the love, power, and wisdom of our Lord. Holley and I face the issues of life together, supporting and loving one another through them. **This is one-flesh life.** Have you experienced this life?

———————————————————————————————————

———————————————————————————————————

I have learned the secret of being content in any and every situation,
whether well-fed or hungry, whether living in plenty or in want.
PHILIPPIANS 4:12

PURSUING CONTENTMENT VERSUS BUILDING DISCONTENT

Our culture trains us to **"never settle for..."** The best life means *high expectations,* and *doing everything possible to get others to meet those expectations*. We have watched this strategy play out over decades in many lives, and see a consistent outcome in "high-expectation" people: chronic discontent. **Do you know a discontented person who is happy and at peace?** These are mutually exclusive. Discontent, in fact, is one of Satan's most powerful tools to lead us away from God's path, to damage lives and relationships. How has discontent—your own or someone else's—impacted your life?

_____

_____

How big a role do expectations play in your life?

_____

_____

To live the best life, what do we need? Think carefully about your answer. John D. Rockefeller, one of the wealthiest men who ever lived, had a simple answer for this question: "Just a little more." **Being discontented with our current circumstances does not drive the universe, God, or other people to fulfill our expectations.** It just makes us unhappy with whatever life we happen to have now. This state of unhappiness will probably continue indefinitely. We may want to see different things in our life. But, when these different things are *in our life* will we be satisfied, or want still more? Are you happy with your life, or unhappy? Why?

_____

_____

We must understand the difference between *aspirations*, which are good, and *discontent*, which is never a good thing. God has us *where we are in life* for a reason. If we only want to be somewhere else, we miss the blessings found here and now.

Do not be anxious about anything, but in every situation, by prayer and petition
with thanksgiving, present your requests to God. And the peace of God which transcends
all understanding will guard your hearts and your minds in Christ Jesus.
PHILIPPIANS 4:6-7

God tells us to be thankful. Why? To shift our attention to the *potential benefit* of a situation, and away from the threat it poses. Can we be thankful and fearful at the same time? Try it sometime. The answer is, "No." God does not want us to remain where we are in life. **He has a far more radical agenda for us than we have for ourselves.** But He wants us to have *a certain quality of life throughout this journey.* The best life experience requires us to be **at peace with our life** as it is, and to be thankful for all that God is doing in our life. How have you seen the power of thankfulness in your life?

_____

_____

CONTENTMENT IN OUR MARRIAGE

Let's apply this same thinking to our husband or wife. A key focus of dissatisfaction in Marriage may be our Covenant partner. He or she may not meet our expectations in one way or many ways. **We may be used to weaponizing our expectations** to "help" others be all they can be—for our sake. This pattern can certainly carry over to our most significant other. In Marriage we may barter approval for expectation-meeting. Which may happen infrequently, if ever. All of us have seen this pattern even if it is not part of our relationship. Is this pattern part of your Marriage?_____

But consider these things. Does God deal with our imperfections in this way? Does the kindness of God lead us to repentance? Does God fully accept us as we are, even though He does not leave us as we are? No one grows to their potential in an atmosphere of harsh disapproval or manipulation. Also, if we are frequently dissatisfied with our mate, **what quality of life are we creating for ourselves?** We are the author of our own dissatisfaction, despite viewing ourselves as the victim of our mate's imperfection. God wants us to enjoy the best possible quality of life—not only when we get better at doing life—which we hopefully will—but here and now. How do we live this better life? **By learning how to be content here and now.** As Paul says in Philippians 4:12, "I have learned the secret of being content..." **What is that secret?**

_____

_____

...God causes all things to work together for good to those who love God...
Romans 8:28

What is "the long view"? We need to learn to *settle for the process,* to be **OK with the way God works,** and with **the way we grow and the pace at which we are both transformed. What is the secret? Contentment is not related to our circumstances. It is a decision we make.** What would it take for you to be content in your Marriage right now?

_____

_____

For the eyes of the Lord range throughout the earth to strengthen
those whose hearts are fully committed to Him.
II Chronicles 16:9

RECOGNIZING OUR PLACE IN THE SPIRITUAL WAR WE INHABIT

We live in a war zone, in our world and in our Marriage, that we did not create and cannot fix. God built within us *a desire for the perfection for which we were originally created.* We long for the perfect world, the perfect life, and the perfect us—that was the Garden of Eden. If we are in Covenant with God, this and more is waiting for us in eternity. But for now *we live here.* We live in a world and in relationships awash in the consequences of the sins of the entire human race. This place is messy on a good day, and capable of far worse. **Yet, joined to God and following His path, we are here for a reason.** God wants to show us that **He has overcome the world,** and **He is capable of overcoming its impact on us if we will follow His path out of the mess.** It never looks perfect on a given day because **it will never be perfect in this place.** Some of this is on us. We all make our contribution to the mess. For now, God wants to teach us how to live the new life He gives us in Covenant. **He wants us to build a Marriage that is a city set on a hill, giving light to all.** He wants us to *learn to transform ourselves by means of His truth,* and enjoy the outcome. He wants us to love others in the way He loves them, which requires that we go to His school of love, that we go through His process of growth and transformation. This plan is *the only way God can reach a lost and dying world through us.* **God looks for those who are willing to receive this life, and those who are willing to faithfully develop it.**

WHY DID GOD CREATE MARRIAGE?

A Marriage is more than a relationship. *It is a reflection of God Himself, of the relationship among the Trinity.* In Marriage we are doing more than seeking our most delightful life; **we are to establish our family as a representation of God and His Kingdom squarely in the middle of this world,** to demonstrate to all the power of God to give new life, then to build this life into something truly worth having. God has a plan to build a life and Marriage worth emulating. **This is His plan for each of our Marriages.** This is why wholehearted devotion to God, His plan, and our husband or wife makes sense. This is why **scrupulous obedience to this plan—and exacting faithfulness to every part of our Covenant**—makes sense. This is why God created us, created Marriage, and placed us right here, right now. And why we should listen very carefully to Him and **consider very carefully what we do going forward** with these wonderful gifts we have been given by the Almighty God.

Unless the Lord builds the house, the builders labor in vain.
Psalm 127:1

Two people are at the altar. **Each has a blueprint in mind for the Marriage.** *Have you ever seen a builder try to build a house using two different blueprints?* What if each blueprint contains misinformation? What if the specs for the foundation are not right, some walls are not properly supported, and some hallways lead to nowhere? God, the master Builder, has a blueprint for Marriage. If we draw from God's plan but still try to graft in parts of our own plan—what are the chances that the most livable and beautiful home emerges from this chaos? Or, would we benefit from selecting one vision from among the contenders, and *one plan* to guide our building process?

What is your vision for your Marriage, and what are you going to do to build this vision?

_____

_____

_____

_____

_____

_____

_____

_____

_____

_____

_____

_____

_____

_____

_____

_____

_____

_____

_____

_____

_____

_____

LESSON TWELVE

HOW GOD'S COVENANT PLAN FUNCTIONS and THE RELATIONSHIP GOD'S PLAN PRODUCES

We have covered a lot of ground in this study. Some of this may be new to you. We have examined many of the moving parts of Marriage and how they fit together. Now, let take these assemble parts and see how they work together.

Whoever has my commandments and keeps them is the one who loves me.
JOHN 14:21

All authority in heaven and on earth has been given to Me. Therefore, go and make disciples of all nations, baptizing them in the name of the Father and the Son and the Holy Spirit, and teaching them to obey everything I have commanded you.
MATTHEW 28:18-19

…the people became more and more unfaithful, following all the detestable practice of the nations…
II CHRONICLES 36:14

…You destroy all who are unfaithful to You.
PSALM 73:27

GOD'S COVENANT PLAN: FAITHFULNESS IN ALL THINGS

There are many parts of Covenant to understand. **But there is one thing God wants to be uppermost in our minds—faithfulness.** Faithfulness is carrying out God's plan in every way, large and small. Our faithfulness puts God's plan into effect. God loves us all, but faithfulness is the response from us that is rewarded by God. What does faithfulness look like for you and me in daily life?

In Christian life we say we want **more faith**. What exactly do we want? First, faith is to believe that God exists, and rewards those who seek Him (Hebrews 11:6). Faith is believing that what God says is true, and that His Word is the definition of truth (John 17:17). Faith is believing *in Him* (John 14:1). Knowing that He loves us, that everything He tells us to do is for our good (Jeremiah 29:11). But faith is more than realizing these things. If we want to be *full of faith*, we want to be *faith-ful, or faithful*. To be truly faithful we must do more than decide that we want to be. **We must build the correct foundation within ourselves to become faithful.** We must *go through the process of growth and transformation* that builds this foundation. This process is the plan within Covenant.

GOD'S GIFT OF LOVE, AND THE INNER CONFLICT IT CREATES

The love we feel for another is one of God's most precious gifts. Marriage joins us in a way that matches our desires. We truly become one. We are changed in a way that *makes it possible to actually love* in every way, now and forevermore. We *vow our total commitment.* Left to our own perceptions and ideas, though, we are caught between our desire to love and *other priorities we have embraced.* Absent God's plan, we give some of ourselves to our Marriage *and some to other things* we are deceived into believing are more important. Thus, we are faced with an insolvable internal conflict. What do we do with deeply rooted things within us which oppose love and faithfulness? God's plan meets us at this point. He offers us *the tools to build and rebuild as He directs.* We must weed out the elements of our being which oppose our love. These things are now *out of sync with who we are, and our relationship with our beloved.* **This is the inner conflict we sign up for at the altar.** A conflict between *our love and other parts of us.* Have you experienced this conflict?

OUR INNER CONFLICT IS PART OF A HISTORY-LONG SPIRITUAL CONFLICT

This inner conflict mirrors the conflict in the spiritual realm that has played out in individual lives and cultures throughout history. **The weapons in this war are ideas, perceptions, and desires.** The battleground is the mind and heart of every person. **The tide of battle turns on one factor—our decisions.** There is a sovereign God behind all of this executing an eternal plan in ways we often cannot perceive. *At stake is the course and quality of our life, the course and quality of our Marriage, and the eternal consequences of our decisions. Also, the lives of our children and the course of our culture* are impacted by every decision each of us makes on a daily basis.

For each of us, this battle comes down to two questions. Is *the idea we are considering* God's truth for our lives? Then a second question. If so, will we embrace it and live it? Or, if it is not God's truth, will we reject it and eject it from our life? Everything else in Marriage is set in motion by our answer to these questions, day after day. How do your daily decisions impact your Marriage?

If one does not understand these underlying spiritual realities *we will not understand the true origin of the problems in our Marriage*, nor **how to overcome** these problems. Instead, we will settle for far less than is possible in Marriage. Or, we simply walk away. Some of these spiritual realities are the definition of darkness; others are the definition of light, love, and truth. Yet, **much confusion has been sown about which is which.** If we **gain clarity about the forces** which exert powerful impacts on us and our Marriage, we can **cut through this confusion** and find our best path. *We can only find the path to the Marriage of our dreams by understanding the power and tactics of our enemy*—**and avoiding his guidance as if our lives depend on it.** How do you distinguish between the voice of the Holy Spirit and the voices of the enemies of God?

Our world is characterized by confusion. *Confusion about what is true and right, and about the path to the best relationship and the best life.* **This** is the battlefield on which we attempt to survive and hope to thrive. Are you ever confused about what to do? Does this help you understand why?_____

Does this understanding point to the path out of our confusion?_____

THE PATH TO INNER PEACE, A FAITHFUL LIFE, AND THE BEST MARRIAGE

If we want to *wholeheartedly* believe God, what must we do? If we want to carry out His plan with single-minded devotion, what must we do? *First, we must face our doubts and areas of confusion head-on.* We must identify the ideas we bought into that question God and the truth of His Word, or its relevance to our lives. We must examine our ideas, *affirm* what is true, and *disaffirm* each lie. *We also must note the things within ourselves that oppose living out these truths.* Again, we must reject lies and lovingly embrace truth. This process removes the obstacles within us to faithfully following God's plan. **Faith is a guidance system built on truth, a character formed on truth, a self-image based on truth, and an understanding of God based on truth—faithfulness is the result.** We can *reasonably obey* God in all things, large and small, because we *know what to do, know why we do these things, and know how we become able to do these things.* This understanding comes from Scripture, and also comes from understanding the nature of our Covenant relationship. *Faithfulness to Covenant and the faith that God blesses are the same thing.* How does this compare with your view of faith?

If we are to be a person of faith, we must fill our minds and hearts (and a regular part of our schedule) with God's truth. We must devote the time necessary to build a relationship with God, just like we must spend time with our husband or wife to build our Marriage. Then, we must simply do life together with God and our spouse. Issues will arise, fights will happen, agendas will clash, priorities will differ. We can fight these things out till only one is left standing—or until we are find ourselves alone. Or, we can approach these issues according to God's plan. **We only learn to love in the context of a relationship.** We can say we love if we are sitting in a room by ourselves. But *we cannot really know what is in our heart, mind, character, and guidance system unless we are in an intimate relationship in our day-to-day life.* **Covenant— Marriage, and a relationship with Himself—is God's ultimate school of love. Love is also the outcome of our faith and faithfulness.**

A LIFE BASED ON TRUTH

Our task in life is to **identify and choose to live out truth.** We are not designed to create, or define, or redefine reality. Our job is to recognize reality and align ourselves with it. This is a challenging task in a world filled with powerful deceptions.

> *…not forgetting what they have heard, but doing it—they will be blessed in what they do.*
> JAMES 1:25

The job is not finished when we correctly identify truth. We must **develop convictions** about foundational things. Then, if we are to live this plan out consistently, we must develop convictions about one element after another of God's plan. Have you developed any new convictions as a result of this study, or identified any you would like to develop?

LIFE: NOT JUST ABOUT RIGHT AND WRONG, BUT ABOUT A PROPER BALANCE

Our powers of Attention and Intention are here for a reason. We must still **sift through competing priorities** to decide where we will focus. For any idea or opportunity, we must decide **what, if anything, we are going to do about it**. The enemy is hell-bent on offering us a "better" use of our time and energy than God's plan. **With each idea, situation, and scenario we must decide.** Our decision unleashes the consequences inherent in our decision. We are always building…something. What have you built in your Marriage thus far, and what do you want to build going forward?

Identifying and implementing truth **reprograms our guidance system.** It also **builds new and stronger character qualities**—faithfulness, determination, integrity, and many other virtues. Over time we travel faster and faster down God's path because our character and guidance system come **more and more into alignment with God's guidance.** Inner struggles fade, replaced by a wholehearted love for our Covenant partner, be it God, and/or a husband or wife. We become capable of singleminded devotion to our partner and relationship. *Our character, guidance system, identity—and our Lord and His truth—are now in harmony.* This leads to new levels of satisfaction, gratification, and peace. God richly rewards faithfulness in the depth of our beings, as well as in our life. Are you experiencing a life of satisfaction? Why or why not?

In this Study Guide we have walked you through the process of building your Marriage on this foundation. Now, you must decide whether or not you will apply this understanding. This is God's path. Or, will you follow the leadership of the world? Some try to draw elements from both plans. But, if you are trying to walk down a path, moving in opposite directions at the same time has a predictable result. What are your thoughts about this question for your life?

THE RELATIONSHIP GOD'S PLAN PRODUCES

What kind of relationship does God's plan produce when lived out? We will draw from personal experience. My relationship with Holley is not perfect. If you are not clear about this, ask her. Neither one of us is perfect—far from it. But over decades of implementing God's plan, understanding Covenant and living out its realities, we have built a relationship so good that we want to write a book about how this can happen. If it happened for us, it can happen for anyone who follows God's path. We have both grown in ways we could have never imagined. We have developed strengths and capabilities in our lives we did not know were possible.

IF LIVES ARE PREPARED, GOD OFFERS OPPORTUNITIES

Along the way, God has brought opportunities before us that matched our new capabilities and strengths. Pursuing these opportunities built more good things within us, which led to further opportunities. If we are faithful, in other words, we enter a life that is correctly described in Ephesians as "abundant, beyond anything we could ask or imagine." This morning Holley and I were discussing the many ways our *lives tap into* every potential and ability we have, as it continues to develop new ones. We and our lives are perfectly matched. Only from the hand of God…. Are you experiencing this kind of match—between *who you have become, who you are as a couple, and your life?*

What qualities are produced by this kind of relationship? Every *aspect of Covenant* and *faithfulness to Covenant* go into producing each quality. *Covenant is a wonderfully interlocking plan,* **dependent on every aspect and every decision.** God does not waste our time or effort; He directs these toward our greatest benefit. Here is a selection of relationship qualities drawn from *The Covenant of Marriage.* We strongly suggest you read the more extensive and detailed list. We all need as clear a vision as possible of what God can do in our lives and Marriages if we allow Him to.

MEETING DEEPEST NEEDS

We learn our own needs and each other's, and learn how to meet each other's needs in substantial ways. Both giving and receiving create profound peace and satisfaction. We are not striving to breathe, barely getting enough air, barely hanging on in a life that is hanging by a thread. **We are full, satisfied by wonderful and nourishing food.** We express our *true* selves and are fully appreciated. Love offered, love received, love returned in ways that touch us most deeply. Happy is too shallow a word to describe what it feels like to be on the receiving end of this kind of love. And it is more blessed to give than to receive such love. Are deep needs being met in your Marriage?

UNCONDITIONAL ACCEPTANCE

This acceptance happened once and for all at the altar. No earning, no ongoing evaluation to see if someone makes the cut. **We are now joined; we are one.** Yet, in many relationships people do not feel *fully accepted.* What is your experience?

RECIPROCITY

Covenant is a giver-giver relationship. Each vows to love in action in every way. Covenant is the ultimate blank check—whatever you need, whatever I have or can become. We learn by experience that it is more blessed to give, more beneficial to build, more delightful to share, and more gratifying to care. If our self-interest includes *another self* (our spouse) and we live this out, we find the joy of being part of something more important than ourselves—a marriage, a family, and the plan of God for humanity. Is this reciprocity part of your Marriage?

HONOR

Our mate bears the image of God. He or she is made in His image (and hopefully contains His Spirit through the New Covenant). We desire respect, and to be worthy of it. **We desire admiration, and want to earn it.** We want someone to think the best of us—and have good reasons for doing so. Covenant instructs us to honor each other. But we are imperfect. We do not always reflect our Maker. We are to spur each other on to better character, more wise decisions, more correct priorities, more decisive actions, and ever more faithfulness to God and His path. As we display honor, we promote honor and build an honorable life. Do you and your spouse support each other in this way?

HONESTY AND TRUST

We are to hear a fair and balanced picture of situations, not a self-serving or manipulative one. **We trust in our partner,** confident that there are no concealed motives or agendas, no secret places in life, no hidden actions. *We are confident that love fills the other's heart for us*—confident of loving intentions and motives. We are in this thing together. *We help and support each other, help the healing process, and promote growth and transformation.* Honesty and trust are the foundation of all of this. What level of honesty and trust is in your relationship?

TRANSPARENCY

To experience being loved for who we are we must know what is down inside us, and be willing to reveal this to another. To discover what is within, we must be willing to be honest with ourselves. We can only do this if we know we will be loved regardless of what we find in the depths of our being. The world tells us we cannot be loved because… So, we learn to hide all the becauses. Even from ourselves. But these very areas and issues—and the lies that drive them—lead to the greatest progress when transformed. Inner conflicts, even if unrecognized, sap our energy. The consequences of a misdirected guidance system are a huge burden for us. **Our tour of the depths of ourselves is not a sightseeing trip, but a hunting expedition—to find and destroy lies, then to plant truth and watch it grow into something beautiful.** Hand-in-hand with God, we transform **what is** into **what should be.**

Willfully blinding ourselves to issues in ourselves **also blinds us to deeper things about our partner.** We can only know another to the depth we know ourselves. During our own (life-long) search, it is good to reveal what is within to our beloved. *This is not "confession-fest," but simply being truthful about deeper things we discover as we move through life*—motivations, dreams, goals, fears, and deepest pains. If we are used to

131

looking at ourselves at deeper levels, we will spot things to adjust in our depths as we working through daily issues. This pattern is the fast-track to personal growth, which better equips us to deal with future issues. If two go through life building themselves in this way, they *grow together.* In a transparent life we enjoy the delight of having every area of life observed and appreciated. What level of transparency is in your relationship? And, is personal growth a pattern in your Marriage?

SAFETY

Marriage is to be a refuge from the world, a place to rest, relax, recover, restore, recharge, rebuild, and replenish. *Our home life must be built with great skill and care to become such a place.* Each must feel safe in the relationship before almost anything else good can be built. Do you feel safe in your home? Why or why not?

SECURITY

This means **safety for the long run** instead of just in the moment. What creates a sense of security? Confidence that **both are committed for the long haul.** "Wisdom" is the term we use for decisions with the best long-term outcome. We are instructed to seek it, for wisdom is of greater value than any material thing. Wisely-managed finances, wisely-developed skills to provide for the family, and wisely-conducted key relationships are important. In Covenant we draw from the wisdom of both people, and from God and His truth. But, no matter how clear-headed our deliberations, we cannot see the future. Unexpected things arise. Our security is ultimately in the hands of a loving God who may teach us an important lesson by allowing a reversal or disaster to visit us. **The most powerful factor in our security is an unshakable trust in God's love**, *coupled with confidence in His long-term plan for us and our family.* Where does your security come from?

PERMANANCE

Love is a remarkably resilient thing, enduring through long periods of separation or the greatest adversity. Love seems an "out of time" thing—*to reside more in the timeless spiritual realm than the here and* *now.* It seems as if we have always known our beloved, and we will always love each other. Our hearts long for the permanence God build into this relationship—"until death do we part," "happily-ever-after," "love-for-a-lifetime." No one celebrates "love-for-awhile." The other is now within us. We can literally never be alone. How does this permanence impact your heart?

_____

_____

INTIMACY

Intimacy is one of the "big" words. Like *love* or *faithfulness*, it is made of many parts and means many things. **It is the experience of being unconditionally loved in light of everything we are, and having our love received by another.** It is "the perfect bond of unity," Colossians 3:14, involving spirit, mind, heart, will, and body. It is **the blending of two hearts on fire for each other,** of *two minds knowing each other at deeper and deeper levels.* It is **two wills devoted to each other above all.** It is **experiencing the literal joining of two spirits.** Physical intimacy begins our Covenant, and is to celebrate it frequently. This physical experience, in turn, draws from and celebrates everything that has been built in the relationship (good and bad, by the way). It is the *experience of intimacy in all its forms* that meets our deepest emotional needs, fulfills our deepest dreams, and gratifies our deepest desires. Plus, we are in communion with God if we are in Covenant with Him. One can simply view *intimacy* as sexual intercourse, but if we do the word loses virtually all meaning. What does intimacy mean to you, and in your Marriage?

_____

_____

WHOLEHEARTED

In single life, often no one sees us closely or clearly enough to help us grow. We maintain our equilibrium by keeping our distance, so other people will not see large parts of us—*the parts we would most benefit from transforming.* **These are our contradictions, our areas of confusion, and our compromises with the world.** These are the ropes pulling us in all directions. *In a Covenant relationship over time these areas will come to light. In a faithfully-conducted relationship these areas will be brought into conformity with truth.* **Thus, our minds, hearts, wills, and lives will receive coherent direction from a single source and move in a single direction.** Inner conflicts, confusing and dysfunctional emotions, and other things that keep us stuck in place in life are replaced by truths that set us free to live our best lives and build our best relationships. We may receive a peace from God that passes understanding, but the peace and harmony produced by harmony of mind, heart, and will **with God, His plan, and our Marriage** is easily understood. We simply stop receiving conflicting and contradictory directions for living from sources at war with each other—**importing this war into our minds and hearts**. This is a huge step toward our best experience of life. What in your life and Marriage are you wholehearted about?

PASSIONATE

If our lives no longer contain a mass of confusion and conflicting directions, **truth has set us free.** To do what? **To pursue our own growth and development.** To find things **within our identity that we were created to do and be.** Talents and gifts become fueled by our emotions. When expressed, these bring delight. Some need to dance, others to paint, or write, or cook, or travel, or take out your gallbladder as elegantly as possible. God's plan is about **learning who we are,** then living it out. God's path, faithfully walked, **produces a series of passions that ultimately fill one's life.** As we experience this life, then consider the Author of all of this, our hearts are inflamed with passion for the One who has made us one and filled our lives with blessings. What are you passionate about in your life?

CONTENTMENT

Contentment is one side of a coin. The other side is honoring God and our mate. *We cannot have one without the other.* This is the doorway through which all good things pass. Discontent blocks this door. An old Chinese proverb says, "For the one who is next to a fire, if he does not appreciate the fire, it is as if he has no fire." We must continually direct our attention toward things for which we can be thankful—or we will miss them. We want to build good things, **but also to learn to fully enjoy these things.** This is a different skill. We must *cultivate an appreciation* for our husband or wife, our Marriage, and our life. Life is full of unrecognized blessings. Eden certainly was. One of Satan's most powerful and effective attacks is to create **a sense of discontent—a desire for more in a life which already has enough,** though *we may not have made the effort to realize it.* The more we understand about something the more we appreciate it—antique watches, food, a good book, your husband or wife—so become a student. Understand what it takes—the effort, planning, creativity, and love—for your wife or husband to do the routine things in life that keep the wheels turning. Be grateful for the small things and the big ones. But be careful: when you reward something with gratitude you will likely get more of it. After all, how many blessings can one person stand? How contented are you with yourself, with your spouse, with your Marriage, and with your life?

FORGIVENESS

We have all gone off the cliff at one time or another, or made compromises that (almost) no one notices. None have followed God, loved, or kept commitments perfectly. Sometimes we really hurt each other. We make a mistake, and something deeply valued is gone forever. In the closeness of Marriage *we will inevitably inflict serious damage on one another.* God's plan is that we learn not to. *Until we achieve perfection (which will not happen on this earth)* there will be a role for forgiveness. But **what is forgiveness?**

It is key to realize **what it is not.** It is not to forget about it, as if the offense was not real or the damage does not matter. It does *not erase the offense,* nor does it *erase all the negative consequences* of the offense. It is not simply to turn and once again open our hearts to the person. **Initially we must recognize several important realities.**

First, our concern is not only the offense and damage. It is also the **risk of future damage** from someone who does not understand how much damage was done, or does not care. Second, we want the person to *assume responsibility* for what they did. This includes *undoing the damage.* Third, an often unrecognized part of the scenario is that *we are all on our journeys, and this scenario is intended by God to teach a lesson—to everyone.* Fourth, God's moral universe is still there. *Negative consequences will still occur to aid the learning process.* Fifth, **it is God that oversees the teaching process for each of us. This is not our role for each other.** So, in light of these things, what is forgiveness?

It is to **lay down our expectation that the offender will make the situation like it never happened.** God is our source of supply. **Let Him restore our damage and heal our heart in His way.** Also, He is *much better* at applying leverage in someone's life than we are—though His sense of timing and ours may not coincide. God says, "Vengeance is mine—I will repay" (Hebrews 10:30). **We do well to get out of His way.** Then, in light of God taking over the role of restoring what is damaged, and overseeing the teaching and consequences, *we are free of the burden of fixing someone else.* Instead of turning our back toward the offender, *we can turn to them with open arms and an open heart,* **knowing that God is our great Protector and Provider.** Perhaps He is also trying to teach us something in the situation; if so, best to not miss that. God adds a nudge of motivation for us to forgive: **if we do not forgive others, neither will He forgive us** (Matthew 6:15).

For the offender, God's plan is repentance. That is, to recognize the fullness of the damage done (by asking and listening carefully). Then searching out the matter in Scripture, going through the guidance-system revision we described (for any such offense is a guidance system issue). The goal is to develop a new conviction about this matter. Living out a new conviction and repairing damage as best one can rebuilds trust.

A necessary asterisk involves criminal or abusive behavior. One must not deal with such things only between the couple—**for forgiveness is often perceived by this type of offender as a green light to repeat dangerous behavior.** One *must* involve a professional third party or the authorities, and avoid enabling dangerous behavior. **Telling the truth and acting in accord with truth is the rule here, not concealing it.** *At times love must be very tough.*

PARTING THOUGHTS

We said at the beginning that Covenant is more than a relationship. It is also a plan. Do you now see why we said this? Many are not aware that God's gift of Marriage comes with a plan attached. Others see God's plan as merely a pile of rules, ones which may not be relevant in our modern world. Some realize Marriage is about love and faithfulness, but cannot find it within themselves to build this kind of relationship. Many have made peace with something far less than their Marriage could be, because they see no path to anything else. If we are deeply in love with someone, we want what people have always wanted—happily-ever-after. But, how can our Marriage become the wonderful thing we all hope it *could* be? This Study Guide has offered a brief look at God's plan to fulfill our dreams for Marriage.

God's plan has many parts that work together to build many things. This plan is not an un-doable list of Scriptural commands. Instead, it is a path that leads us toward a destination. We cannot see where our path leads or what this journey holds for us at the outset. We will not know this until we walk the path. In the beginning, we can only *trust in* the source of our directions—the One who walks with us as we travel. Our deepest hope is that you decide to trust this plan and its Author—to the point that you are willing to walk with Him down this path. Though not always fun and never easy, this is a journey that makes life truly worth living.

The centerpiece of God's plan is *our transformation and joining*. Everything else we are to do depends on something *God does* as we enter the Covenant of Marriage. Scripture tells us that *He joins us together* as "one flesh," changing our identity and nature in the process. *Everything we are to do simply brings our way of life into harmony with our new nature and bond.* We grow the new life we have become much like we grew our initial life—discovering and developing new capacities along the way. We build and re-build our character and guidance system. The intent of all of this is that we develop the capacity to consistently love others in action through all the circumstances of life. Our personal growth allows us to fall more deeply in love with our beloved year after year. We learn to more deeply appreciate the love of our life, and our life with our beloved. We build the best Marriage as we build the best *us*.

Sadly, not everyone follows God's plan. Even those who attempt to follow Him do so imperfectly. Fortunately, perfection is not the goal. The other centerpiece of God's plan is *faithfulness*. This is not perfection. Instead, faithfulness means to make the choice to follow God's path with each step. Then, if we are mistaken or deceived and move in the wrong direction, to acknowledge our mistake and take corrective action. The corrective action inherent in Covenant is about far more than simply making a new decision next time. It is about evaluating and revising our beliefs, changing our guidance system, and building our character. If we do this, the mistake we made becomes *something we would never do* even if given the opportunity. God's goal is not perfect behavior, or even loving behavior. It is that our lives become an authentic expression of the *new life and relationship* He has given us, both of which reflect God Himself. *His life* is characterized by love, virtue, obedience, and blessing. Or, we can choose to keep building our old, separate, single life—the life that no longer exists.

We face the choice to follow God many times a day. The choice to build God's life is made more difficult by our own reluctance and resistance—which comes from competing ideas we embraced as true. Ideas that are no longer true, if they ever were. Our decisions are also complicated by the conflicting voices we hear in our culture. To follow God we must declare our independence *daily* from our culture, from forces trying to re-fashion our God-created world in the image of another leader. We must daily affirm our belief in God and our trust in His love. Then, we use the three powers God placed within us to live out our convictions, hand in hand with the Living God.

We hope you have gained a new understanding of God's plan and a new vision for your Marriage during this brief introduction to Covenant—*the heart of God's plan for your life, and for all of humanity.*

May God's choicest blessings be yours!
Holley and Mark Johnson

ENDNOTES

LESSON ONE

1. *Covenent*; Kay Arthur, Precepts International, Chattanooga, Tennessee.

2. *The Blood Covenant, A Primitive Rite and Its Bearing on Scripture*; H. Clay Trumbull, Zondervan, second edition (1958—originally published in 1885)

LESSON FOUR

3. Wedding Paper Divas, from WeddingPaperDivas.Nearlyweds.com, accessed May 2019

4. Merriam Webster Online Dictionary, www.Merriam-Webster.com/, accessed May 2019

LESSON SIX

5. *Evidence that Demands a Verdict,* Josh McDowell, Thomas Nelson and Co., Nashville, Tn. 1979

6. *New American Standard Bible,* Zondervan, 2018

7. *Sex and Eroticism in Mesopotamian Literature,* Gwendolyn Lieck, Chapter 14, et. al; Routledge, NY 2003.

LESSON NINE

8. "What was I Thinkin'"… Deric Ruttan, Brett Beavers, Dierks Bentley; recorded by Dierks Bentley, Capitol Records, Nashville, 2003

9. *The 5 Love Languages: How to Express Heartfelt Commitment to Your Mate,* Gary Chapman, Northfield Publishing, 1992

OTHER BOOKS IN THE COVENANT SERIES

MARK JOHNSON, MD and HOLLEY JOHNSON, MS, RDH

The best defense of Biblical Marriage in our generation!
…and the best case for faithfulness, the foundation for Revival!

WHAT IS A COVENANT? Rather than a CONTRACT (the current teaching), COVENANT is entered via *an exchange of identity* with another. The two are joined by *a bond of identity,* and *the identity of each is altered*—the "one flesh" bond of Marriage, or a new creature indwelled by the Holy Spirit. Covenant is not just a tie that binds. Inherent **in the nature and structure of Covenant is a Plan— that is all about love, and all about faithfulness.** We are told to love; taught God's definition of love; offered many new motivations to love; and transformed—so that we become able to love deeply and consistently across the spectrum of life and relationship…if we follow God's plan.

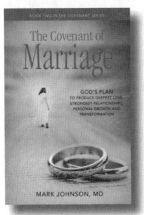

THE COVENANT OF MARRIAGE Join us as we examine *God's Covenant plan for Marriage.* First, the nature of Marriage—the **exchange of identity** as we enter it and **the bond that is formed.** Then, the implications of the *transformation* that occurs as we wed. God's intends that we **shift our way of life**—*our decisions, values and priorities*—into accord with the reality of our nature and our relationship. We examine how this is done, and the quality of relationship this shift produces. In addition to creating the best relationship, this approach produces the best version of us. Which, in turn, allows us to build the best possible life.

THE NEW COVENANT (March 2021) Once in Covenant with God, *who have we become, and what are we supposed to do?* The answers are found in the nature, structure, and function of a Covenant. We are *new beings* in a *new bond with God, indwelled by His Spirit.* Love and obedience are the native language of this new being, and the commands of our Lord But, this authentic life is opposed by a guidance system we acquired from *the world.* By *transforming our mind,* this guidance system can change. We *put off* the external life produced by our old guidance system, and *put on* an external life that authentically expresses the being we have become—we **live up to** what **we have already attained.** God's foremost commands are to love—Him, and others. His Covenant plan is designed to produce *faithful people*, capable of loving Him and others across the spectrum of human experience…*if we follow God's plan.*

ABOUT THE AUTHORS

Dr. Johnson has focused on personal spiritual growth, mentoring, and teaching for over forty years. Following his introduction to the historic understanding of Covenant in a Kay Arthur Bible study in 1983, his efforts integrated around *the nature of His relationship* with God, and his marriage, understanding he terms, "the most important single thing I have ever learned in my life before God." Mark and Holley not only built spiritual lives upon this foundation, but also their marriage—field testing these concepts and approaches while raising seven children and building a very multifaceted life together. The two built a medical practice which draws patients from 49 states and many foreign countries. Dr. Johnson is a teacher, mentor, and researcher in his specialty. Mark and Holley want to share the things they have found most important in life—things they are convinced represent *the very heart of God's plan for each of us, and for all of us.*

MarkJohnsonMDAuthor.com
FB: @CovenantBook,
@MarkJohnsonAuthor